Valmouth

A Musical

Sandy Wilson

A SAMUEL FRENCH ACTING EDITION

SAMUEL FRENCH

FOUNDED 1830

SAMUELFRENCH-LONDON.CO.UK
SAMUELFRENCH.COM

ISBN 978-0-573-08061-6

www.samuelfrench-london.co.uk

www.samuelfrench.com

VALMOUTH

First performance at the Chichester Festival Theatre on
19th May, 1982, with the following cast of characters:

Mrs Hurstpierpoint	Judy Campbell
Nit, the footman	Richard Freeman
Mrs Thoroughfare	Jane Wenham
Father Colley-Mahoney	Frank Shelley
Sir Victor Vatt	Terence Conoley
Grannie Tooke	Doris Hare
Carry	Cathryn Harrison
Madam Mimosa	June Bland
Lady Parvula de Panzoust	Fenella Fielding
Lady Saunter	Liza Hobbs
Mrs Yajñavalkya	Bertice Reading
David Tooke	Robert Meadmore
Thetis Tooke	Cheryl Kennedy
Dr Dee	Richard Evans
Niri-Esther	Femi Taylor
ffines, the butler	Lockwood West
Sister Ecclesia	Marcia Ashton
Fowler	Sue Withers
Captain Dick Thoroughfare	Mark Wynter
Lieutenant Jack Whorwood	Simon Butteriss
Cardinal Pirelli	Robert Helpman
Inhabitants of Valmouth	Amanda Wise
	Sue Withers
	Michael Anthony
	Simon Beresford
	Gregor Hausmann
	Adrian Smith
	Simon West

Directed by John Dexter
Musical direction by John Owen-Edwards
Orchestrations by Richard Holmes

Synopsis of Scenes

Time—the period of Ronald Firbank

SONGS

ACT I

No.	Song	Performer
No. 1	**Valmouth Prelude**	Dr Dee, Thetis
No. 1A	**Valmouth Opening**	Sir Victor, Grannie Tooke, Lady Parvula, Company
No. 2	**Magic Fingers**	Mrs Yajñavalkya
No. 3	**Mustapha**	Mrs Yajñavalkya
No. 4	**I Loved A Man/What Den Can Make Him Come So Slow?**	Thetis, Niri-Esther
No. 5	**I Loved A Man** (Reprise 1)	Thetis
No. 7	**All The Girls Were Pretty**	Lady Parvula, Mrs Thoroughfare, Mrs Hurstpierpoint
No. 9	**What Den Can Make Him Come So Slow?** (Reprise)	Niri-Esther
No. 10	**Just Once More**	Lady Parvula
No. 12	**Lady Of The Manor**	Niri-Esther
No. 14	**What Do I Want With Love?**	David
No. 15	**Big Best Shoes**	Mrs Yajñavalkya
No. 15A	**Big Best Shoes** (Reprise)	Mrs Yajñavalkya
No. 17	**Niri-Esther**	Captain Dick Thoroughfare, Lieutenant Jack Whorwood
No. 19	**Cry Of The Peacock**	Mrs Yajñavalkya, Niri-Esther

ACT II

No.	Song	Performer
No. 21	**Little Girl Baby**	Mrs Yajñavalkya
No. 23	**Cathedral Of Clemenza**	Cardinal Pirelli, Company
No. 24	**Only A Passing Phase**	Lady Parvula
No. 25	**Valmouth** (Reprise)	Captain Dick Thoroughfare
No. 26	**Where The Trees Are Green With Parrots**	Niri-Esther
No. 27	**My Talking Day**	Sister Ecclesia
No. 27A	**My Talking Day** (Reprise)	Sister Ecclesia
No. 28	**I Will Miss You**	Mrs Yajñavalkya, Grannie Tooke
No. 31	**Where The Trees Are Green With Parrots** (Reprise)	Niri-Esther
No. 32	**Finale**	Company

The Vocal Score and Orchestral Parts to *Valmouth* are available on hire from Samuel French Ltd.

The lyrics of the songs are reproduced by kind permission of Noel Gay Music Co. Ltd.

ACT I*

SCENE 1

The Road to Valmouth. An early summer afternoon

As the Lights come up, the music of Valmouth is heard

No. 1 Prelude

Dr Dee (*off, singing*) Valmouth!
Thetis (*off, singing*) There's no air to compare with the air . . .
Valmouth . . .!

As in the Novel:
Day is drooping on a fine evening in March as a brown barouche passes
through the wrought-iron gates of Hare Hatch House on to the open highway.
Seated behind Nit, the footman, who is driving the coach, is a lady no longer
young, Mrs Hurstpierpoint. Her fragile features, long and pointed, are
swathed, quasi-biblically, in a striped Damascus shawl that looks Byzantine, at
either side of which escapes a wisp of red, crimped hair. By her side reclines a
plump, placidish person, Mrs Thoroughfare, whose face is half concealed
beneath a white-lace coal-scuttle hat. Facing the ladies a biretta'd priest,
Father Colley-Mahoney, appears to be perusing a little fat, greasy book of
prayers which he holds aslant so as to catch the light

Mrs Hurstpierpoint (*poking Nit with her parasol*) Benighted idiot!

Nit turns round

Didn't I say, blunt-headed booby, to Valmouth?
Nit To Valmouth?
Mrs Hurstpierpoint By way of Fleet. (*To Mrs Thoroughfare*) Pardon,
Thoroughfare, you were saying?
Mrs Thoroughfare Evil, evil, evil. Nothing but slander, wickedness and lies.
N'est-ce pas, Father Colley?

Father Colley-Mahoney is buried in his prayer-book

Mrs Hurstpierpoint What is your book, Father Colley-Mahoney!
Father Colley-Mahoney Saint Stanislaus-Kostka, my child.
Mrs Thoroughfare Kostka! It sounds like one of those islands—those
savage islands, where my darling son Dick stopped at once, just to write
to his old mother.

---

*N.B. Paragraph 3 on page ii of this Acting Edition regarding photocopying and
video-recording should be carefully read.

Mrs Hurstpierpoint Where is he now, Eliza?

Mrs Thoroughfare Off the coast of Jamaica; his *ship*——

She is interrupted by a man's voice, off

David (*off, shouting*) To heel! Bad dog!

A dog barks

Mrs Thoroughfare It's that crazy shepherd. David Tooke—the brother, you
know, of that extraordinarily extraordinary girl.

The dog barks

David (*off, further away*) Doucey boy!

Father Colley-Mahoney (*to Mrs Hurstpierpoint*) How—how if the glorious
Virgin required you to take this young fellow under your wing?

Mrs Hurstpierpoint For the sake, I presume, of his soul?

Father Colley-Mahoney Precisely.

Mrs Hurstpierpoint But is he ripe?

Father Colley-Mahoney Ripe?

Mrs Hurstpierpoint I *mean* . . . (*She breaks off, rather confused*)

Mrs Thoroughfare (*to cover the silence*) I—I trust we shall be in Valmouth
before Wilks the Haberdasher closes. I did require a ribbon—a *roughish*
ribbon . . .

Father Colley-Mahoney When was Mrs Wilks a hundred?

Mrs Thoroughfare Only last week.

Mrs Hurstpierpoint Nowadays around Valmouth centenarians will soon be
as common as peas.

Mrs Thoroughfare The air, there's no air to compare to it!

Father Colley-Mahoney (*contemptuously*) Valmouth air, Valmouth air.

Mrs Thoroughfare (*carried away*) At the *Strangers' Hotel* it seems there's
not a single vacant bed. Victor Vatt, the delicate paysagiste came
yesterday, and Lady Parvula de Panzoust was to arrive today.

Mrs Hurstpierpoint I was her bridesmaid many years ago—and she was no
girl then.

Mrs Thoroughfare She stands, I fear, poor thing, now, for something
younger than she looks.

Father Colley-Mahoney Fie, Thoroughfare!

Mrs Thoroughfare Fie, Father?

Mrs Hurstpierpoint (*softly*) La jeunesse—hélas—n'a qu'un temps.

Mrs Thoroughfare (*ecstatically*) Oh, but the air, the air!

The Lights fade

SCENE 2

The Market Square, Valmouth. Early that evening

*High on a column in the middle of the square stands the "virile, but
rudimentary" statue of "John Baptist Daleman, b. 1698, ob. 1803, Valmouth's*

illustrious son." At the back, R, *is the façade and entrance of the* Strangers' Hotel. L, *the churchyard and the tower of St Veronica's.* DR, *the Nook, Mrs Yajñavalkya's cottage. Above the doorway hangs a sign:* Mrs Yajñavalkya. Masseuse and Chiropodist. *Opposite,* L, *is the doorway and windows of a farmhouse, outside which is a sign saying:* Tooke's Farm. *The Nook should be built in such a way that it can be swung open to reveal the interior when required*

When the Lights go up, Sir Victor Vatt, a distinguished-looking elderly gentlemen, is seated at his easel at the base of the Daleman statue, painting a view of St Veronica's. He takes up the melody of "Valmouth" and sings the number, joined gradually by other inhabitants: Grannie Tooke, leaning out of the farmhouse window, Madam Mimosa, the town's only demi-mondaine, Carry, Mrs Yajñavalkya's little English maid, Mrs Hurstpierpoint, Mrs Thoroughfare and Father Colley-Mahoney

No. 1A. Valmouth Opening

Sir Victor
Valmouth!
There's no air
To compare with the air
Of Valmouth.
There's no light
That's so bright as the light
Of Valmouth.
On the banks of the Val.
Circled by the friendly hills
Sheltered by the sky,
Safe are we from wordly ills
Time that kills
Passes us by
In Valmouth
Every care
Seems to fade in the air
Of Valmouth
There's a balm
To be found in the calm
Of Valmouth, on the banks of the Val.
Come and spend a while with us
And learn to sigh and smile with us.
And when you leave it,
Strange as it seems,
Valmouth stays in your dreams.

All
Though the season is barely beginning,
The town is already a-hum.
By coach and car
From near and far
The visitors simply come and come.

There are some who are here for the first time

	And some who appear every year.
Granny Tooke	I hate the lot
	But if they've got
	Some money to spend, they're welcome here.
	I have seen them come and go
	For more years than I care to remember.
	Oh the fancy folk that have come and gone,
	How glad I'll be when they've all moved on
	Come September.
All	Come September.
	But the season is barely beginning,
	The town's in a ferment of fuss,
	And every nook
	And cranny's took.
Granny Tooke	Cranny's took?
All	Yes, Grannie Tooke!
	And we can see
	It's going to be
	A wonderful season for us.

Lady Parvula de Panzoust enters from Strangers' Hotel. *She is of uncertain age, elaborately gowned and coiffured. She greets Sir Victor*

Sir Victor (*speaking*) Welcome back to Valmouth, Lady Parvula.
Lady Parvula (*speaking*) Thank you, Sir Victor.
Sir Victor (*speaking*) And how is London?

Lady Parvula (*singing*)	Oh London is simply exhausting,
	It leaves you more dead than alive.
	But now that I'm once more in Valmouth
	Already I start to revive.
	Society life is so tiring.
	It leaves you quite rinsed out and wrung.
	But now that I'm once more in Valmouth
	I'm suddenly wonderfully young.
All	It's, the air, it's the air,
	It's the beautiful Valmouth air.

Lady Parvula (*speaking*) Well whatever it is, it's doing wonders for me.

All (*singing*)	Valmouth!
	There's no air
	To compare with the air
	Of Valmouth.
	There's no light
	That's so bright as the light
	Of Valmouth.
	On the banks of the Val.
	Circled by the friendly hills
	Sheltered by the sky,
	Safe are we from worldly ills

> Time that kills
> Passes us by
> In Valmouth
> Every care
> Seems to fade in the air
> Of Valmouth
> There's a balm
> To be found in the calm
> Of Valmouth, on the banks of the Val.
> Come and spend a while with us
> And learn to sigh and smile with us
> And when you leave it,
> Strange as it seems,
> Valmouth stays in your dreams.

Lady Parvula (*speaking*) Eulalia! Elizabeth!

Mrs Hurstpierpoint
Mrs Thoroughfare } (*together*) Parvula!

Mrs Thoroughfare So you have arrived safely! How good to see you again.

Mrs Hurstpierpoint And how well you look. To be continually beautiful like *you*, dear. How I wish I could ...

Lady Parvula Yet I date my old age from the day I first took the lift at the Vatican.

Mrs Thoroughfare And where is your daughter, Gilda?

Lady Parvula Gilda ... Gilda's training under Luboff Balza—in Milan.

Mrs Hurstpierpoint To what end?

Lady Parvula Music. And she is in such cruel despair. She says Luboff insists on endless counterpoint, and *she* only wants to play waltzes.

Mrs Hurstpierpoint She hardly sounds to be ambitious.

Father Colley-Mahoney coughs

Oh, dear Father, forgive me. (*Introducing them*) Lady Parvula de Panzoust, Father Colley-Mahoney.

Father Colley-Mahoney (*taking her hand and bowing*) Dominus vobiscum.

Lady Parvula How charming. (*To Mrs Hurstpierpoint*) So, you've lost Father Ernest?

Mrs Hurstpierpoint Alas! He preferred flitting about the world like you.

Lady Parvula I go about, as other fools in quest of pleasure, and I usually find tedium.

Mrs Hurstpierpoint We must try and help you to avoid it whilst you are in Valmouth. Will you dine at Hare Hatch House tomorrow evening?

Lady Parvula I am all anticipation!

They are interrupted by mysterious strains of oriental music apparently coming from the Nook. Everyone in the Square turns towards it

The front door opens and Mrs Yajñavalkya appears in the doorway

Everyone looks at her, particularly Lady Parvula

No. 2 Magic Fingers

Mrs Yajñavalkya   Good-evening, good-evening,
(singing)   It certainly is a most entrancing evening.
    This early Valmouth spring is such a pleasure for me,
    Although I fear it's not a time of leisure for me,
    For spring can be a source of such insidious ills,
    Like nervous strains,
    And stomach pains
    And libberish chills.
    So I hope dat you will bear with me
    In case de point applies,
    If I take dis opportunity
    To advertise.
(Speaking) Ladies, if you are suffering from any ob de following disorders:
(singing)   Neuritis, fibrositis,
    Colitis or arthritis
    Lumbago or a little touch of gout,
    Bronchitis, hepatitis,
    Cystitis or phlebitis
    Or just a tendency to getting stout,
    Or any kindred ailment
    Dat dis flesh ob ours is heir to,
    Den ladies I'd be happy
    To enrol you if you'd care to
    Undertake a course ob me
    For my new inclusive fee.
    Here's my card.

She hands out cards. Lady Parvula takes one and reads it

Lady Parvula   "Mrs Yajñavalkya—"
    That's the most bizarre of names.
    Can she really do
    Such wonders as she claims?
Mrs Yajñavalkya *(speaking)* I'd be happy to prove it, milady, to you.
Lady Parvula *(speaking)* We shall see. But tell me, Mrs Yajñavalkya, what is your secret?
Mrs Yajñavalkya *(speaking)* My secret? Why it isn't any secret. It's a well-known fact
(singing)   Dat
    I've got magic fingers,
    Where I touch de magic lingers,
    And dose ebil spirits fly.
    If all your pain and misery you'd banish,
    Den come to me and wiv a touch
    I'll make dem vanish.
    Wiv my magic digits

I can soothe your aches and fidgets,
And I safely prophesy
If you care to try me,
You will find I'm speaking true.
For I've got magic fingers,
Let my magic fingers
Work dair magic spell on you.

(*Speaking*) Ladies, I am also an expert in:
(*singing*)   Cometics, dietetics,
Obstetrics and emetics,
And other rather esoteric skills,
And I possess prescriptions
Of numerous descriptions
For balms and balsams,
Lozenges and pills,
And if you've any problem
Dat requires a special knowledge
I've also a diploma
From an eastern ladies' college
Dat entitles me to sell
Aphrodisiacs as well.
Here's my card.

She laughs as everyone scrambles for a card

I've got magic fingers
Where I touch de magic lingers,
And dose ebil spirits fly.
If all your pain and misery you'd banish,
Den come to me and wiv a touch
I'll make dem vanish.
Wiv my magic digits
I can soothe your aches and fidgets,
And I safely prophesy
If you care to try me,
You will find I'm speaking true.
For I've got magic fingers,
Let my magic fingers
Work dair magic spell on you.
And you, and you, and you, and you, and you, and
you!

Mrs Yajñavalkya goes back into the Nook. Grannie Tooke disappears from the window

Mrs Hurstpierpoint Tomorrow evening, Parvula, eightish . . . Just the three
of us—and Father Colley of course. Come, Elizabeth . . .
Lady Parvula Too much bliss!

Mrs Hurstpierpoint goes, followed by Mrs Thoroughfare and Father Colley-Mahoney

Lady Parvula catches sight of Madam Mimosa

Lady Parvula So! Er—Madam Mimosa!

Madam Mimosa (*surprised at being addressed by her*) Yes, milady?

Lady Parvula Madam Mimosa, I wonder ... I wonder if our oriental masseuse is not quite what she seems.

Madam Mimosa What *do* you mean, milady?

Lady Parvula Only that she might be setting up, if that is how one puts it, a rival establishment to your own.

Madam Mimosa (*suddenly common*) Well, I'll be——

Lady Parvula Oh, my dear girl, it's just a thought. And in any case a little friendly competition might *ease your burden*. After all, you have held the monopoly in Valmouth for so *many years*.

David comes out of the Nook and crosses to Tooke's Farm. Granny Tooke looks out of the window

Granny Tooke David! Any orders?

David Mrs Yaj wants a boiler. And extra butter at the hotel.

Granny Tooke Be sure to say it's risen. Butter and eggs have gone up. And while you're at the hotel, you might propose a pair of pigeons or two—to the cook.

Grannie Tooke disappears

David moves C. Lady Parvula crosses his path and pretends to see him for the first time

Lady Parvula Oh!

David Good-evening, ma'am. (*He moves*)

Lady Parvula I—er ...

David Yes, ma'am?

Lady Parvula I wonder if you could tell me the way to the—er—the *cathedral*?

David The cathedral ... Bain't no cathedral round these parts, so far as I know. But (*pointing to the church*) that be St Veronica's.

Lady Parvula St *Veronica's*—how sweet—such a *helpful* girl. Thank you, good fellow.

David It's no trouble, ma'am. No trouble at all.

David exits

Lady Parvula Oh ... *Quel joli garçon!* Quite—as Byron said of d'Orsay—a "*cupidon déchaîné*" ... Such a build. And such a voice! (*She laughs delightedly*) He must be mine ... in my manner ... in my way ... I always told my dear late lord I could love a shepherd—peace be to his soul!

Lady Parvula exits

Granny Tooke (*off*) Thetis! Thetis!

Grannie Tooke comes out of the farmhouse

Fetch out my chair. It's time for Mrs Yaj to come to give me a massage.

Thetis follows her out with a chair

Oh, if only I could get about the place as once I did!

Thetis Maybe with warmer weather here you will. This very night the old sweetbrier tree came out. The old sweetbrier! And none of us thought it could.

Granny Tooke Don't let me hear you talk of thinking. A more feather-brained girl there never lived.

Thetis I often think, at any rate, I was born for something *more brilliant than waiting on you.*

Granny Tooke Impudent baggage!

Thetis goes into the house

Make ready my thingummies. Mrs Yaj is coming!

Dr Dee crosses the Square towards St Veronica's, carrying a wreath

(*Contentedly*) Hey-sy-ho, it's good to be still alive!

Mrs Yajñavalkya comes out of the Nook and crosses over to Grannie Tooke

Mrs Yajñavalkya And how do you find yourself today, Mrs Tooke?

Granny Tooke To be open with you, Mrs Yaj, I feel today as if all my joints want oiling!

Mrs Yajñavalkya Oh, it will pass ... I shall not let you slip through my fingers: Oh no; your life wif me is so precious.

Granny Tooke I can't hope to last very much longer, Mrs Yaj, anyway, I suppose.

Mrs Yajñavalkya That is for me to say. How is your young grand-daughter's erot-o-maniah, Mrs Tooke? Does it increase?

Granny Tooke God knows, Mrs Yaj, what it does.

Mrs Yajñavalkya We Eastern women never take lub serious. And why is dis, Mrs Tooke? Because it is so serious!

Granny Tooke Love in the East, Mrs Yaj, I presume, is only feasible indoors?

Mrs Yajñavalkya Nobody bothers, Mrs Tooke. Common couples wif no place else often go into de jungle.

Granny Tooke Those cutting winds of yours must be a bar to courting.

Mrs Yajñavalkya *Our* cutting winds! It is *you* who have de cutting winds ... It is not us ... No; oh no. In de East is joy, heat!

No. 3 Mustapha

Granny Tooke (*speaking*) Then where do those wicked blasts come from?

Mrs Yajñavalkya (*speaking*) Never you mind now, Mrs Tooke, but just cross does two dear knees ob yours, and do wot I bid you ... (*She sings*) Oh Allah la illaha. (*Speaking*) I shall have you soon up and about again, I hope, and den you shall visit *me* ...

(*Singing*)   Oh you must come and see
My blossoming acacia tree.
We'll sit and talk and watch de blossoms fall.
And later on you'll taste.
My peaches and my cherries,
And when de winter comes,
You'll see my holly berries.
Oh holly is my favourite of dem all.

Granny Tooke (*speaking*) Holly, Mrs Yaj?
Mrs Yajñavalkya (*speaking*) Yes, holly, Mrs Tooke.
(*Singing*)   For every time I see
De holly on de bough,
I think of my late husband
And how
Dat beard ob his would prickle
Just like de holly on de bough.

Granny Tooke (*speaking*) Your late husband, Mrs Yaj?
Mrs Yajñavalkya (*speaking*) That's right, my dear.
Granny Tooke (*speaking*) And what did you say his name was?
Mrs Yajñavalkya   His name was
(*singing*)   Mustapha, Mustapha,
What a man was he!
Mustapha, Mustapha,
Was all de world to me.
His kisses were like wine,
Like wine from de finest vine,
And when he commenced caressing
Lordy, I don't mind confessing
Paradise was mine—
Can you imagine?
Mustapha, Mustapha,
How my cup would fill
If my beloved Mustapha
Were with me still.

He had a way of singing songs to me
Whenever I was feeling sad.
And when he told me "You belongs to me."
I'd tell him "Honey, I is glad."
He had a way of making love to me
I've never known before or since.
Dat man to me was
A lion. Yes he was
A prince.

His name was Mustapha, Mustapha
What a man was he!
Mustapha, Mustapha,
Was all the world to me.

His kisses were so sweet,
Without dem I'm incomplete.
Every time dat man would stroke me
My poor heart was like to choke me,
You could hear it beat!
Can you imagine?
Mustapha, Mustapha,
How my soul would thrive,
If my beloved Mustapha
Were still alive, Were still alive!

(*Speaking*) Of course he was a debil!

Thetis comes out of Tooke's Farm

Granny Tooke (*seeing her*) Howsomever! Where are you off to, so consequential?

Mrs Yajñavalkya Dat enlarged heart of hers should be seen to, Mrs Tooke. Do persuade her now to try my sitz-baths. I sell ze twelve tickets ver' cheap—one dozen for only five shillings.

Granny Tooke That won't cure her of idiocy.

Mrs Yajñavalkya What idiocy, pray, dear lady?

Granny Tooke She thinks she's going to marry young Dick Thoroughfare.

Mrs Yajñavalkya And become mistress of Hare Hatch? (*Enigmatically*) Oh, she thinks that, do she?

No. 4 I Loved A Man/What Den Can Make Him Come So Slow?

Thetis   I loved a man and he sailed away
Ah hé, ah hé.
He left me here and away he's gone,
My heart is there in the ship he's on
Ah hé, ah hé, ah hé.

So here I sit at the end of day
Ah hé, ah hé.
To watch the tide as it flows to sea
And ask the waves where my love can be
Ah hé, ah hé, ah hé.

He promised me so faithfully
That I would be his wife.
If he should break his oath,
I'll take my life.

I loved a man and he sailed away
Ah hé, ah hé.
He sailed away on the ocean main
And here I wait till he comes again
Ah hé, ah hé, ah hé . . .

Mrs Yajñavalkya (*speaking contemptuously*) Mrs Richard Thoroughfare,
Mrs Dick, Mrs Thorough Dick . . .! (*She crosses to the Nook*)

Niri-Esther appears at the upper window of the Nook

(*Ecstatically*) Mrs Niri-Fairy . . . Mrs Niri-Fairy Thorough-Fare—of
Hare Hatch House . . .!

Niri-Esther   Here am I with arms that ache for him,
(*singing*)   Why they're aching he ought to know.
                Ev'ry night I lie awake for him.
                Wot den can make him come so slow?

                All day long I sit and sigh for him,
                I'm still sighing when lights are low.
                Don't he know I'd gladly die for him?
                Wot den can make him come so slow?

                Wot is he doing?
                Wot is he saying?
                Is he on dry land or sailing the sea?
                If he's my true love,
                Why's he delaying
                To come back home to me?
                Oh, why den don't he come back home to me?

                Well he knows dat he means more to me,
                More dan mortals can ever show.
                When we kissed goodbye, he swore to me
                We'd be together soon but oh . . . oh,
                Wot den can make him come so slow . . . slow?

Thetis   I loved a man and he sailed away
                Ah hé, ah hé, ah hé . . .

Thetis wanders off

Niri-Esther sighs and continues to gaze out of the window

David enters

Granny Tooke David!
David Coming, Grannie!
Granny Tooke Where's your sister got to?
David Thetis?
Granny Tooke Ay. I'll be wanting my supper.
David She's likely down by the river.
Granny Tooke River? And what takes her there, may I ask?
David Who knows? I'll fetch her home.

David exits and Grannie Tooke goes back into the farmhouse

The Lights fade

SCENE 3

The Banks of the River Val. A little while later

Thetis is heard singing, off

David enters

David (*calling*) Thetis! Thetis! Where be 'ee? (*He hears her singing, and moves over to the other side*) Thetis!
Thetis (*off*) H'lo?
David Come in now!
Thetis (*off*) I shan't.
David Come in, Thetis!
Thetis (*off*) I won't. I will not.
David You'll catch your death!
Thetis (*off*) What of it?
David (*angrily*) Thetis!
Thetis (*off*) Oh, all right. I'm coming.

Thetis enters. The hem of her dress is wet, and so are her legs and feet

David You've been standing in the river again
Thetis What if I have?
David What do you stand there for?
Thetis Well ... when the tide flows up from Spadder Bay I pretend it binds me to the sea. Where my sweetheart is. My—betrothed.
David Your betrothed? You mean Captain Dick?
Thetis Who else?
David 'Od! You're a simple one, you are!
Thetis Me?
David Yes, you.
Thetis (*pleading*) Don't be horrid, David, to me ... You mustn't be. It's bad enough quite without. What with Granny——
David She'll not be here for long.
Thetis I don't think she'll die just yet.
David (*looking up at the sky*) It's a cruel climate.
Thetis Ay, cruel.
David Now you'd best come home. Granny is in a regular fury with 'ee.
Thetis Oh, give me just a few minutes. Then I'll come. I promise.
David All right. (*He moves off*) Douce, boy! Douce!

David exits

No. 5 I Loved A Man (Reprise 1)

Thetis   I loved a man and he sailed away
(*singing*)   Ah hé, ah hé.
                     He sailed away on the ocean main
                     And here I wait till he comes again
                     Ah hé, ah hé, ah hé ...

The Lights fade

SCENE 4

Hare Hatch House. The next evening

The façade of the manor house, in front of which can be set such furniture as is required. At the present moment this is the dining-table, laid for four, with chairs

When the Lights come up, ffines, the elderly butler, and Nit, the footman, are putting the finishing touches to the arrangements—polishing the cutlery, lighting the candelabra, etc.

ffines (*dropping some cutlery*) Dash it!

Nit You seem to be in quite a state tonight, Mr ffines. Is anything the matter?

ffines The matter, George?

Nit Go on, tell us.

ffines I'd sooner tell me beads. Put your fork straight . . . Where were you at teatime by the way?

Nit Father Colley-Mahoney sent for me again.

ffines Again? I should have thought once was enough. What did he say to you?

Nit "*Veni cum me in terra coelabus!*"

ffines Hm! On the whole I preferred Father Ernest.

Nit And so did half the maids.

ffines Although his brilliance here was, as you may say, wasted.

Nit 'Pon my word! It's a deadly awful place.

ffines With the heir presumptive so much away it's bound to be slow and quiet.

Nit Why the captain should be heir of Hare I never could make out!

ffines Mr Dick's dead father, Admiral Thoroughfare, was a close relative of Mrs Hurst. Indeed, they might have married . . . Only he was too poor. And things fell out otherwise.

Nit There'd be a different heir, I s'pose, if missis married ag'in?

ffines Hardly likely. Why, she'll soon be a centenarian herself.

Nit What a lady! You've only to change her plate to feel she's there.

ffines So I should hope!

Nit And as to Father Colley. My! How he do press!

A sound of wheels and horses' hooves off L

ffines There's Lady de Panzoust's cab. Run and meet her, and be sharp about it!

Nit runs off L

ffines gives the table a final check

Nit ushers on Lady Parvula who is in elaborate evening dress

Lady Parvula Please tell the cabby to return for me at ten o'clock.

Nit bows and goes off

Good-evening, ffines. Nobody about?

ffines (*taking her wrap*) The mistress, I presume, is with the scourge.

Lady Parvula (*to herself*) Poor Eulalia! Still mortifying the flesh at her age. (*To ffines*) Tell me, ffines, is it true that she sometimes assumes spiked garters?

ffines As to that, milady, I couldn't say. But Fowler reports that she wears a bag of holly leaves pinned to the lining of her gown ... Will that be all, milady?

ffines bows and withdraws

Lady Parvula As for me, it would take more than a scourge to keep *my* flesh in check! Oh, the very thought of that shepherd sets me in a ferment. Tomorrow I shall tax the negress ...

Mrs Thoroughfare enters, wearing white, "all billowing silks and defenceless embroideries"

Mrs Thoroughfare Parvula! Welcome once more to Hare!

They kiss

Lady Parvula Why Elizabeth, tonight you look positively *jeune fille*!

Mrs Thoroughfare I always say that there is no joy like the coolness of a white dress after the sweetness of confession.

Lady Parvula What news do you have from Dick?

Mrs Thoroughfare No letters lately, naughty boy, but a crate of some wonderful etherized flowers came from him only this afternoon, from Ceylon.

Lady Parvula Even at Oomanton certain of the new hybrids this year are quite perfect.

Mrs Thoroughfare Eulalia and I often speak of the wonderous orchids at Oomanton Towers.

Lady Parvula We're very proud of a rose-lipped one, with a lilac beard.

Mrs Hurstpierpoint enters wearing a loose, shapeless gown of hectically contrasted colours

Mrs Hurstpierpoint A lilac *what*?

Lady Parvula Eulalia!

Mrs Hurstpierpoint Is it Sodom?

Lady Parvula (*tittering*) Goodness no!

Mrs Hurstpierpoint Because Father Colley won't hear of it ever before dessert.

Lady Parvula How right.

Mrs Hurstpierpoint He seems to think it quite soon enough. (*Putting her arm round Lady Parvula's waist*) Dearest Parvula, how jolly to have you with us again. (*To Mrs Thoroughfare*) Was it you, Betty, before office I heard amusing yourself in Our Lady?

Mrs Thoroughfare I am sure, Eulalia, I forget.

Lady Parvula After the Sixtine Chapel, I somehow think your chapel is the one I prefer.

Mrs Hurstpierpoint You *dear* you! You should have been with us Easter Day! Our little basilica was a veritable bower of love.

Lady Parvula Have you any more new relics?

Mrs Hurstpierpoint Only the tooth of St Automona Meris, for which I've had my tiara-stones turned into a reliquary.

ffines enters. Nit follows

ffines Dinner is served, madam.

Mrs Hurstpierpoint Thank you, ffines.

The ladies seat themselves

   During the following ffines and Nit come and go serving the first course

Lady Parvula I adore dining *en petit comité*.

Mrs Hurstpierpoint Where can Father be?

Mrs Thoroughfare He went to the carpenter's shop, Eulalia, to give "a tap or two", as he said, to your new prie-dieu.

Lady Parvula While we are alone, you must tell me all the gossip of Valmouth.

Mrs Hurstpierpoint There is not, I fear, much to tell. If I recollect, the cattle show was our last gaiety.

Lady Parvula Your pathetic, curious oxen ... it's a breed you don't see everywhere! My husband, my Har-e-ee tried them in the park at Oomanton Towers: but they didn't do.

Mrs Thoroughfare No?

Lady Parvula They got leaner and leaner and leaner and leaner in spite of cakes and cakes and cakes and cakes ...

Mrs Hurstpierpoint You should consult local advice.

Lady Parvula It's what I intend doing.

Mrs Thoroughfare I suppose the town is full of imaginary invalids, *comme toujours*?

Lady Parvula My dear, one sees nothing else. So many horrid parliament men come here apparently purely to bask.

Mrs Thoroughfare Men, men ...! "They are always there", dear, aren't they, as the Russians say?

Mrs Hurstpierpoint Nowadays, a man ... to me ... somehow ... Oh! He is something so wildly *strange*.

Mrs Thoroughfare Still, some men are ultra-womanly, and they're the kind I love!

Lady Parvula I suppose that none but those whose courage is unquestionable can venture to be effeminate?

Mrs Thoroughfare It may be so.

Lady Parvula It was only in war-time, was it, that the Spartans were accustomed to put on perfumes, or to crimp their beards?

Mrs Hurstpierpoint My dear, how your mind seems to dwell upon beards!

No. 7 All The Girls Were Pretty

Lady Parvula	Beards! Beards! A beard is a thing I adore.
(*singing*)	But a beard that is really a beard
	One just doesn't see any more.
Mrs Thoroughfare	Moustaches! Moustaches! That's what I chiefly miss,
	For mustachios
	Add *quelque chose*
	To a kiss.
Mrs Hurstpierpoint	I was always keen on whiskers,
	For I found in the last resort
	If you held a man by the whiskers,
	He was well and truly caught.
All	But we're sad to say
	That the men today
	Are a dull clean-shaven lot.
Lady Parvula	And the men we loved have all passed on,
	Like the world we knew they are dead and gone.
All	And we sometimes wonder what
	To do with the world we've got.
Lady Parvula	It only seems like yesterday
	When life was like a song.
Mrs Hurstpierpoint	And all the girls were pretty
Mrs Thoroughfare	And all the men were strong.
	The world appeared a better place
	Where nothing could go wrong
Lady Parvula	For all the girls were pretty
Mrs Hurstpierpoint	And all the men were strong.
All	The sun was always shining
	In a bright blue sky above
	And we were always frantic'lly
	Romantic'lly
	In love.
Mrs Hurstpierpoint	That other time, that other place,
	Is where we all belong
Mrs Thoroughfare	Where all the girls were pretty
Lady Parvula	And all the men were strong.
	Do you remember Coco ffoulkes?
Mrs Thoroughfare	Flossie St Vincent and Bimbo Stookes?
Mrs Hurstpierpoint	Twirly Rogers and Bushy Ames?
	They all of them had such expressive names.
Mrs Thoroughfare	And the Duke of Crewe on a great black nag
	In hunting pink with the Valmouth Drag.
Lady Parvula	And Monkey Trotter in guardsman's rig
	Doing a rather suggestive jig.
Mrs Hurstpierpoint	And Princess Zoubaroff who came to stay
	And changed her tiara
All	Twice a day!

Lady Parvula	And Laura van Hoof with her purple hair
	Who once ran nude through the Market Square.
Mrs Hurstpierpoint	And Bungy Sussex—the Earl I mean—
	Who used old brandy as brilliantine.
Lady Parvula	And Violet Logg, who eloped with a sheik
All	And was always drunk during Holy Week!
Mrs Thoroughfare	How fine they were!
Lady Parvula	How sublime they were!
Mrs Hurstpierpoint	How great and grand in their prime they were!
All	They were bold and beautiful, brave and true,
	And it goes without saying that we were too.
	The sun was always shining
	In a bright blue sky above
	And we were always frantic'lly
	Romantic'lly
	In love.
	That other time, that other place,
	Is where we all belong
	Where all the girls were pretty
	And all the men were strong.
	Where all the girls were pretty
	And all the men—
Lady Parvula	Ah then, the men—!
All	Yes all the men were ... (*They sigh*)

Father Colley-Mahoney comes in. He coughs

Mrs Hurstpierpoint (*recollecting herself*) With a *dominus vobiscum!*

Father Colley-Mahoney bows to the ladies, mumbles a grace and seats himself

ffines enters, followed by Nit carrying the wine

ffines (*to Lady Parvula*) Lulu Veuve? Veaujolais? Clos Voulksay? Or Château-Thierry?

Lady Parvula If only not to be too like everyone else, *mon ami*, you shall give me some of each.

Nit pours her wine

How incomparable your livery is!

Mrs Hurstpierpoint It has a seminary touch about it, though at Headquarters it's regarded (I fear) as inclining to modernism, somewhat.

Lady Parvula Pray, what's that?

Mrs Hurstpierpoint Modernism? Ask any bishop.

Lady Parvula I once—I once peeped under a bishop's apron!

Mrs Hurstpierpoint Oh ...?

Mrs Thoroughfare And whatever did you see?

Lady Parvula Well ... I saw—I saw ... the dear bishop!

Father Colley-Mahoney (*coughing disapprovingly*) Apropos, his Eminence writes that he may be visiting this country before too long.

Mrs Thoroughfare The dear Cardinal! He must stay here with us!

Lady Parvula Which Cardinal do you speak of?

Mrs Thoroughfare Why, Cardinal Pirelli of course! (*Confidentially*) He owes, they say, to women at least half of his red hat . . .

Father Colley-Mahoney (*reprovingly*) Thoroughfare!

Sister Ecclesia dances rapidly on and off

Lady Parvula Oh!

Mrs Hurstpierpoint What is it, Parvula?

Lady Parvula I thought I saw a figure, in a nun's habit, dancing between the cypresses.

Mrs Hurstpierpoint That will be Sister Ecclesia. She comes from the Convent of Arimathea at Sodbury.

Lady Parvula So? But why is she dancing?

Mrs Thoroughfare She was always over-talkative, so the Abbess imposed upon her a Vow of Silence. She is only allowed to speak three times a year.

Lady Parvula Poor creature!

Mrs Hurstpierpoint The rest of the time she expresses herself in movement—even dancing.

Sister Ecclesia appears again and dances off

Mrs Hurstpierpoint Parvula, you're tasting nothing. For my sake allow Dr Dee of Valmouth to systematically overhaul you.

Lady Parvula Dr Dee? To tell the truth, I was thinking of visiting Mrs Yajñavalkya.

Mrs Thoroughfare Really, Parvula? When?

Lady Parvula Tomorrow . . . perhaps . . .

Mrs Hurstpierpoint (*coldly*) Shall we take coffee in the drawing-room? It grows a trifle chilly out here.

She rises and the others follow suit

Lady Parvula After your super-excellent champagne, I feel one ought to go with bared feet in pilgrimage to your chapel and kindle a wax light or two.

Mrs Hurstpierpoint My dear, I believe you've latent proclivities!

Lady Parvula I? Never! But, I'm agog to see the tooth of St Automona Meris—do you imagine she ever really ate with it?

Mrs Hurstpierpoint Are you coming, Elizabeth?

Mrs Thoroughfare In one moment, Eulalia; I must speak to Father first.

Mrs Hurstpierpoint (*moving off with Lady Parvula*) Don't, dear, desert us!

Mrs Hurstpierpoint and Lady Parvula exit

Mrs Thoroughfare (*after a moment, to make sure the others are out of earshot*) Do you think, Father, she suspects?

Father Colley-Mahoney (*shaking his head*) Rest assured, my poor child.

Mrs Thoroughfare heaves a sigh of relief

Your confession to me tonight exceeds belief.

Mrs Thoroughfare (*on the verge of tears*) Oh, my darling son, how *could* you!

Father Colley-Mahoney My poor child try not to fret.

Mrs Thoroughfare It makes one belch, Father—belch.

Father Colley-Mahoney They're joined irremediably, I understand?

Mrs Thoroughfare From what he writes I conclude the worst.

Father Colley-Mahoney Won't you show me what he says?

Mrs Thoroughfare (*taking a card from her bosom*) The card is covered, I fear, by the chemicals that were in the crate, gummed to the stem, as it was, of a nauseating lily.

Father Colley-Mahoney Decipher the thing, then, to me—if you will.

Mrs Thoroughfare (*reading it with the aid of a lorgnon*) "These are the native wild flowers of my betrothed bride's country. Forgive us and bless us, Mother. Ten thousand loves to you all."

Father Colley-Mahoney Oh, wretched boy!

Mrs Thoroughfare Oh, Father.

Father Colley-Mahoney That ever any black woman should perform the honours at Hare!

Mrs Thoroughfare (*mirthlessly*) Black? Well—if it comes to that Eulalia herself tonight is more than grubby . . .!

The Lights fade

SCENE 5

The Nook. The following afternoon

Lady Parvula comes out of the Strangers' Hotel, *in day costume, limping artificially. She goes to the Nook and knocks on the door. Carry, the maid, answers*

Lady Parvula Good-afternoon. I have an appointment.

Carry Oh yes, m'm. Will you come in?

Lady Parvula (*coming in and looking round*) Thank you.

Carry Is it for the douche, m'm? Or shall I start the stream?

Lady Parvula Not on my account . . .

Carry curtsies and goes

There are voices off: Mrs Yajñavalkya and Niri-Esther in argument

Niri-Esther (*off*) Yabya!

Mrs Yajñavalkya (*off*) Wazi jabur?

Niri-Esther (*off*) Ah didadidacti, didadidacti.

Mrs Yajñavalkya (*off*) Kataka mukha?

Niri-Esther (*off*) Ah mawardi, mawardi.

Mrs Yajñavalkya (*off*) Jelly.

Lady Parvula (*listening intently*) A breeze about their jelly! (*She looks out of the window*)

Mrs Yajñavalkya enters

Mrs Yajñavalkya Have I not de satisfaction of addressing Milady de Panzoust?
Lady Parvula (*taken by surprise*) I—I believe you do chiropody?
Mrs Yajñavalkya Dat is a speciality ob de house. Vot is dair so important? Oh, when I consider de foot . . . it bear de burden ob ten thousand treasures . . .! Kra!

No. 9 What Den Can Make Him Come So Slow? (Reprise)

Niri-Esther   Well he knows dat he means more to me,
(*off, singing*)   More dan mortals can ever show.
                         When we kissed goodbye, he swore to me
                         We'd be together soon, but oh . . .! Oh . . .!
                         Wot den can make him come so slow?
                         Oh! Oh!
Lady Parvula Perhaps—sometimes—it carries charms.
Mrs Yajñavalkya Dat is my little niece, Niri-Esther.
Lady Parvula She sounds as if she is—in love?
Mrs Yajñavalkya In love?

Lady Parvula sits down and Mrs Yajñavalkya takes off her shoes

Lady Parvula I sometimes see call here a young tall man with his dog.
Mrs Yajñavalkya He call only to fetch de fowls dat flit across to my acacia tree from de farm.
Lady Parvula Is that all?

No. 10 Just Once More

Mrs Yajñavalkya (*singing*) He's awfully choice, my lady.
Lady Parvula   I suppose he is.
Mrs Yajñavalkya   Oh yes, he's awfully awfully choice,
                          And I can tell you his physique is
                          Like the finest type of Greek is,
                          And there's honey in the murmur of his voice.

                          Oh yes he's choice, my lady.
Lady Parvula   Well one knows he is.
Mrs Yajñavalkya   He's quite enough to make my lady's heart rejoice,
                          And I can promise you dat man is
                          Just as brown and strong as Pan is,
                          In other words, my lady,
                          He's choice.
Lady Parvula   Then perhaps you could arrange a rendezvous for me,
                          Somewhere safe——
Mrs Yajñavalkya   I have the very spot in mind!
                          You can meet beneath my blossoming acacia tree,
                          And a safer place you couldn't hope to find.
                          The shepherd boy I'll undertake to bring to you,
                          Say between the hours of three o'clock and four.

And my little Niri I shall tell to sing to you
Some sweet love song or a passage from Tagore.
You should hear her recitations from Tagore.

Lady Parvula   But I shouldn't——
Mrs Yajñavalkya   He's awfully choice, my lady.
Lady Parvula   No I shouldn't.
Mrs Yajñavalkya   So very choice, my lady.
Lady Parvula   Oh I shouldn't. No I shouldn't.
                       But I shall!

Just once more,
Though I'm audacious and I know it,
I would like to chuck my bonnet just as far as I can
    throw it,
And I want to fascinate another man
Just to show my friends and enemies I can.

Just once more,
Before I have to throw the sponge in,
I would like to cast convention to the winds of
    Heaven and plunge in—
To a love affair with everything *en place*,
Which will probably provide my *coup de grâce*.

Oh the urge
That still manages to emerge
From this all too willing flesh that I inhabit.
Is there something wrong with me
If I now appear to be
Just a still-seductive,
Non-productive,
Rabbit?

Though I swore,
When my late husband coughed his soul out,
I would try to stop the beast in me from throwing
    self-control out,
Now I find myself confronted with a lad,
Though he mayn't compare with many that I've
    had,
I'm unable to combat the need to add
To my score
Just one more.

Mrs Yajñavalkya (*speaking*) And so you shall my lady, so you shall—
beneath my blossoming acacia tree.
Lady Parvula (*speaking*) Oh I was thinking of that merely as a preliminary.
I would prefer the climax to occur indoors.
    (*Singing*)   Just once more

I want to put my *déshabillé* on,
While I flutter round the room like some *désorientée*
    papillon,
Slapping on strategic rouge and spraying scent
Where so much expensive scent already went.

Just once more,
Ere Father Time applies his sickle,
I would like to prove myself in one celestial slap and
    tickle,
Which will probably result in lord knows what,
But at least I'll use the assets I've still got.

And I'm game
For whatever he cares to name,
For my motto's always been "no harm in trying"—
Though it's likely, I suppose,
I may not survive the throes,
Still I'll sink with my
Libido high
And flying.

And I'm sure
That if the fates decides to claim me,
While a few may sing my praise, there'll be a
    multitude to blame me.
But whatever they may say, they can't deny
That it must have been a lovely way to die,
And upon my tombstone let them carve that I
Cried "Encore!"

(*Speaking*) Just once—too often.

Mrs Yajñavalkya Do you care to undergo a course ob me? For de full
course I make you easy terms; and I always try to end off wiv a charming
sensation.

Lady Parvula Massage, merely as sensation, does not appeal to me—and
otherwise, thank you, I'm perfectly well.

Mrs Yajñavalkya I gib a massage lately to de widowed Duchess ob
Valmouth for less!

Lady Parvula (*standing up*) I always admired her. You'd almost say she was
a man.

Niri-Esther is heard off, humming plaintively

She sounds as if she is crying.

Mrs Yajñavalkya She cry for a sting ob a wasp dat settle on her exposed
bosom. I tell her—at de window—she shouldn't expose it. (*Calling off*)
Fanoui ah maha?

Niri-Esther (*off*) Tauroua ta.

Mrs Yajñavalkya Yahya.

Lady Parvula What's that she says?
Mrs Yajñavalkya That she will be glad to make music for you at any time.
Lady Parvula That will be delightful.
Mrs Yajñavalkya And I also will endeavour to have a few fugitive fowls over from de farm, and you and your beloved shall attain Nirvana.
Lady Parvula Nirvana?
Mrs Yajñavalkya Leave it to me, and you and he shall come together.

David comes out of the farmhouse

David (*calling his dog*) Douce! Hey, Doucey-boy!

Lady Parvula is riveted

Mrs Yajñavalkya He's awfully choice.
David Douce, Doucey boy!

David moves off

Mrs Yajñavalkya He's awfully, awfully choice.
Lady Parvula *C'est un assez beau garçon.* (*She opens the front door, goes out and looks after David*)

Mrs Yajñavalkya watches her

Lady Parvula goes off in the opposite direction

Mrs Yajñavalkya laughs softly

Niri-Esther comes in, carrying a pink kite

Niri-Esther Chakrawaki–wa?
Mrs Yajñavalkya (*turning and looking at her*) Mrs Dick, Mrs Dick Thoroughfare!
Niri-Esther Suwhee?
Mrs Yajñavalkya Mrs Captain Richard Thoroughfare of Hare Hatch House! With her kite!

No. 12 Lady of the Manor

Niri-Esther   When I'm the lady of the Manor,
(*singing*)   I'll do exactly as I please.

Mrs Yajñavalkya goes, laughing

While Niri-Esther sings the scene changes to Hare Hatch House

Hare Hatch House! Hare Hatch House!
Was dere ever a name so fine?
When de man I love comes home from de sea,
Den de world will know dat his bride is me.
And soon very soon
Hare Hatch House will be mine!

When I'm de lady of de manor,
I'll do exactly as I please.

I'll filly my tummy with cakes and sweets,
I'll keep monkeys and parakeets,
Plant de garden with oleander trees.

I'll build pagodas in de paddock
And raise an idol on de lawn.
I'll paint dat manor house pink and white,
Sleep all morning and every night
Have a party with dancing till de dawn.

I shall order turtle soup for my breakfast,
Den I'll feed it to a white Persian cat.
I shall ride around de park on a panther,
Wearing nothing but a great enormous hat.

When I'm de princess in de palace,
I'll ask the King and Queen to dine.
And dere'll be music in every room,
Lights will glitter and flow'rs will bloom,
I'll be happy and life will be divine,
When dat old manor house is mine.
All mine!

SCENE 6

Hare Hatch House. A little while later

Mrs Hurstpierpoint and Mrs Thoroughfare are seated. Mrs Thoroughfare is reading. Thunder and lightning

Mrs Hurstpierpoint Oh-h, the awful vividness of the lightning.
Mrs Thoroughfare Let us go, shall we both, and confess?
Mrs Hurstpierpoint My dear, in my opinion, the lightning's so much more ghastly through the stained glass windows!
Mrs Thoroughfare Dear mother was the same. Whenever it thundered, she'd creep under her bed, and make the servants come and lie down on top ... Poor innocent! It was during a terrific thunderstorm at Brighton that several of the domestics fell above her head ... And the fruits of that storm, as I believe I've told you before, Eulalia, are in the world today.
Mrs Hurstpierpoint My dear, every time the weather breaks you must need hark back to it.
Mrs Thoroughfare (*offended*) Well *I* intend to pray.
Mrs Hurstpierpoint Who knows but our prayers may meet?

Mrs Thoroughfare leaves in a huff

A flash of lightning and a clap of thunder. Mrs Hurstpierpoint clutches her beads and prays feverishly

Love me even as I do Thee, and I will land Thee a fish! I will hook Thee a
heretic, a thorough-going infidel. And so I will make Thee retribution for
the follies of my youth.

*She pauses with her eyes closed, waiting for another clap of thunder, but the
storm appears to have died down*

(*Calling*) Fowler!

Fowler enters

Fowler Yes, m'm?

Mrs Hurstpierpoint Is the worst of the storm over yet, Fowler, do you
consider?

Fowler Now that the wind has deprived the statues of their fig leaves, 'm, I
hardly can bear to look out.

Mrs Hurstpierpoint Unless the summer quickly mends, the Centenarians'
Ball must be postponed!

A clap of thunder

Holy Virgin! Lift the lid of the long casket—and pick me a relic.

Fowler (*going*) Any one in particular, 'm?

Mrs Hurstpierpoint No; but not a leg-bone, mind! And, Fowler! Some
books to read to me, Fowler: Père Pujol for preference.

Fowler goes

A flash of lightning

(*She prays again*) Yes dear Lord, I promise faithfully. A ripe heretic . . .
my little kitchen maid, perhaps . . . I could certainly force her. Or—yes,
I'm sure she has proclivities, she could be shaken—Lady Parvula . . .!

Fowler enters, carrying the relic and some books

Fowler hands the relic to Mrs Hurstpierpoint, who clutches it

Fowler Will *Stories of the Saints* suit, 'm?

Mrs Hurstpierpoint Anything, anything, so long as it doesn't refer to Hell
fire.

Fowler (*opening the book and reading*) "St Automona di Meris became a
boon companion of the Blessed St Elizabeth Bathilde, who, by dint of
skipping changed her sex at the age of forty and became a man."

Mrs Hurstpierpoint A *man*! Don't speak to me of *men*. Especially one of
that description! (*Pointing to the floor*) What is that I see which Mrs
Thoroughfare has been reading? I *know* she's worried! I *know* she's
keeping something from me! What is the book in any case?

Fowler *The Tales from Casanova*, 'm.

Mrs Hurstpierpoint (*about to disapprove, then changing her mind*) Well, well,
for St Francis' sake, an Italian story is always permitted at Hare.

Fowler (*reading*) "There was once upon a time two sisters, who lived with a
certain Madame Orio, in the city of Venice. The disposition of these fair
Venetians was such that—such . . .

Mrs Hurstpierpoint Their disposition? Yes? It was such . . .? That?
Fowler Well, I declare!
Mrs Hurstpierpoint How often, Fowler, must I beg you not to employ that ridiculous phrase in my hearing?
Fowler Very good, 'm, but it's all Portuguese to *me* . . .!

She shows Mrs Hurstpierpoint the book. Mrs Hurstpierpoint reads a little then hands it back

Mrs Hurstpierpoint I see. Well go on.
Fowler "One evening, while Madame Orio was fast asleep in her little belvedere——"

Mrs Thoroughfare enters, leading Sister Ecclesia by the hand

Mrs Thoroughfare Tea-time, Eulalia! I've brought Sister Ecclesia for a cup.
Mrs Hurstpierpoint Oh very well. Thank you, Fowler, that will be all.

Fowler bobs and goes

I did not expect you to finish your prayers so soon, Elizabeth.

ffines enters with the tea-tray which he sets down beside Mrs Hurstpierpoint

Thank you, ffines. Liza dear . . .
Mrs Thoroughfare Yes, Eulalia?
Mrs Hurstpierpoint Whilst we are waiting for the tea to draw, pray give us a few soft bars on the piano. My nerves are all a-jangle.
Mrs Thoroughfare Certainly, dear.

Mrs Thoroughfare goes

Mrs Hurstpierpoint And, ffines, if anyone else calls, better simply say I'm out.

ffines bows and goes

Piano music, "The Centenarians' Waltz", is heard off. Mrs Hurstpierpoint sits back and closes her eyes. Sister Ecclesia begins to sway in time to the music and after a moment or two goes into a dance. She moves out into the garden. Suddenly the pink kite bobs into view. At first Sister Ecclesia does not see it, then she happens to look up and notice it. She looks off to see who is flying it and starts in surprise. She runs back to Mrs Hurstpierpoint, mouthing soundlessly, and clutches at her arm. Mrs Hurstpierpoint opens her eyes and looks where she is pointing

Elizabeth! Elizabeth!

The music stops

Mrs Thoroughfare comes in

Mrs Thoroughfare What is it?
Mrs Hurstpierpoint Look! Someone with a kite is on our lawn!
Mrs Thoroughfare (*looking; in a horrified whisper*) No!

Mrs Hurstpierpoint In the old days sailing a kite heavenwards was my utmost felicity.
Mrs Thoroughfare (*in a low voice*) This is no Christian and her kite, Eulalia.
Mrs Hurstpierpoint No Christian, Elizabeth?
Mrs Thoroughfare It's a savage!

At this moment, Niri-Esther appears holding the kite string. She sees the ladies, hesitates in embarrassment, then laughs.

Mrs Hurstpierpoint (*clasping her beads delightedly*) Oh, Lord, I thank Thee! Thou hast sent me an infidel!

The Lights fade

Scene 7

The Road to Valmouth. Later

David enters

No. 14 What Do I Want With Love?

David   I never saw the countryside so green,
(*singing*)   It looks as if the rain has washed it clean,
                   And everything I see
                   Is like a friend to me,
                   And not a blessed mortal on the scene.

                   When there's the clover that grows in the meadow
                   And the clouds flying by above
                   And a nearby stream
                   Where the fishes gleam,
                   What do I want with love?

                   When there's the song of the lark in the morning
                   And the coo of the turtle dove,
                   And I hear the tale
                   Of the nightingale,
                   What do I want with love?

                   What fools they be
                   Whose hearts are never free!
                   I'm glad I'm me,
                   With a heart of my own
                   As I walk alone

                   Through the clover that grows in the meadow
                   With the clouds flying by above,
                   There is naught I miss

When I have all this.
So what do I want with love?

Mrs Yajñavalkya enters with her doctor's bag. She is out of breath

Mrs Yajñavalkya (*calling to him*) Oh, Mr Tooke! I've been on the outskirts of town, visiting a ruined stomach! I should be obliged, Mr Tooke, if you could one day come to my garden bringing some manure for my little grape house. Manure is what my vine sadly needs.

David I could come tomorrow maybe.

Mrs Yajñavalkya I would be dat grateful, and so, let me tell you, would a certain lady.

David A lady?

Mrs Yajñavalkya Ob aristocratic lineage.

David I han't much time for ladies, Mrs Yaj.

Mrs Yajñavalkya Why, Mr Tooke, wiv your assets you should make time. Otherwise they'll go all to waste!

David Well . . . I'll see.

Mrs Yajñavalkya You *will* see, and you won't, I promise, regret it! (*To herself*) Oh Allah Ilaha, if I cannot throw dem both together, be it only out ob doors, I will be obliged to quench lub's feber wif a sedative.

Mrs Yajñavalkya goes

David	What fools they be
(*singing*)	Whose hearts are never free!
	I'm glad I'm me
	With a heart of my own
	As I walk alone

Through the clover that grows in the meadow
With the clouds flying by above,
There is naught I miss
When I have all this.
So what do I want with love?

The Lights fade as—

David goes

SCENE 8

The Market Square. The next day

The Lights come up on Grannie Tooke who is at the window of Tooke's Farm. She is wearing a new bonnet

Mrs Yajñavalkya enters

Mrs Yajñavalkya Your grandson, Mrs Tooke, seems insensitive to women, I think, my dear, he never has truly enmeshed.

Grannie Tooke He's unimpressionable, I'm thankful to say.

Mrs Yajñavalkya I know ob one lady who would like to impress him. Perhaps tonight at the Ball I could confront him wif her.

Grannie Tooke Oh, the Ball! Tomorrow I shall be as stiff as a rusty hinge.

Mrs Yajñavalkya Den you must wear you feather boa as de nights are chilly.

Grannie Tooke I wish I possessed a great ermine wrap, Mrs Yaj. That is something I've always fancied.

Mrs Yajñavalkya Dair are other furs besides ermine, Mrs Tooke. Wot is dair smarter dan a monkey's tail trimmed in black lace?

Grannie Tooke Belike. But monkeys are scarce around these parts, and in any case I've grown too old for too many doodads.

Mrs Yajñavalkya You too old? Not while you is one ob my clients, dear Mrs Tooke.

Grannie Tooke You old black bogey, what should I do without you?

Mrs Yajñavalkya laughs

Thetis comes out of the hotel, carrying an empty basket. She looks, as usual, very woebegone

(*Seeing her*) It's a hard thing, Mrs Yaj, to be dependent on a wench who spends half her time in the river! If *I* was a fish, I'd snap at her legs. (*To Thetis*) Have you been crying again?

Thetis What if I have?

Grannie Tooke You'll not die in an old skin if you fret it so, Thetis girl, ah, that ye won't.

Thetis What's the use of living in any case, unless you're happy?

Grannie Tooke Come now, belike tonight, at the Ball, we'll both have a bit of a fling.

Mrs Yajñavalkya Dere is nothing so exhilarating as a social occasion, and dat's wot I always say ...

No. 15 Big Best Shoes

(*Singing*)

Any time dey ask me out
To a dinner or a rout
I accept wiv great alacrity,
For perhaps you may have heard
I am quite a flighty bird
And an evening out appeals to me.
What's de reason, do you ask me,
Dat I thus react?
Well de reason if you ask me
Is de simple fact
Dat

I like dressing up
For an evening ball
Or a social brawl

In a fancy shawl
And a silly frilly frock,
And my big best shoes
Go nicka-nacka-nock
Nicka-nacka-nock
Nicka-nacka-nock.

I love dressing up
In my finest clothes
With my beads and bows
And a scarlet rose
On my silly frilly frock,
And my big best shoes
Go nicka-nacka-nock
Nicka-nacka-nock
Nicka-nacka-nock.

I stick a purple or blue
Feather or two in my hair.
What do I care if de people stare?
Den from my jewellery case
Every space I just fill
Till I am glittering fit to kill.
Oh, de thrill when
I start dressing up.
Though my corsets creak,
I am on a peak,
Cos I feel so chic
In my silly frilly frock,
And my big best shoes
Go nicka-nacka-nock
Nicka-nacka-nock
Nicka-nacka-nock.

Dance chorus

I start dressing up,
Though my corsets creak,
I am on a peak,
Cos I feel so chic
In my silly frilly frock,
And my big best shoes
Go nicka-nacka-nock
Nicka-nacka-nock
Nicka-nacka-nock.
Knock! Knock!

No. 15A Big Best Shoes (Reprise)

Tap dance chorus

Nicka-nacka-nock
Nicka-nacka-nock
Nicka-nacka-nock.
Knock! Knock!

Mrs Yajñavalkya and Grannie Took exit

Fade to Black-out

SCENE 9

The Gardens of Hare Hatch House. That evening

There are ornamental shrubs, formal flowerbeds and statuary. Branches are festooned with fairy lights. A swing, twined with flowers, hangs from a tree. From off R *comes the sound of music, dancing and conversation*

No. 16 The Centenarians' Waltz

As the Lights come up one or two couples are strolling around, and ffines and Nit are passing back and forth with refreshments

Mrs Hurstpierpoint, decked in wonderful pearls like Titian's "Queen of Cyprus" and carrying a muff, enters leaning on the arm of Sir Victor Vatt. Father Colley-Mahoney and Mrs Thoroughfare follow behind

Mrs Hurstpierpoint It puts me in mind of Vauxhall when I was a girl . . .
Sir Victor It is so generous of you, Mrs Hurst, to throw open your doors every year. I hope the townsfolk appreciate it.
Mrs Hurstpierpoint Oh, I am sure they do. And I of course find it an excellent opportunity for dispensing holy propaganda. (*She takes a few leaflets from her muff and scatters them around*)
Sir Victor Indeed?

Mrs Yajñavalkya enters with Niri-Esther

Mrs Hurstpierpoint (*listening to the music*) Ah! "The Centenarians' Waltz". How many more times, I wonder, shall I hear it?

She dances with Sir Victor, humming the tune. They dance off and, as they pass Mrs Yajñavalkya and Niri-Esther, Mrs Hurstpierpoint throws down a leaflet

Niri-Esther picks up the leaflet and reads it

Mrs Thoroughfare Poor Eulalia! Her years are beginning to tell on her.
Father Colley-Mahoney Not at all. She'll last in *saecula saeculorum*!
Mrs Thoroughfare Her great regret, you know, she is—God forgive her— the former Favourite of a King: although, as she herself declares, *only* for a few minutes. Poor darling! She gave herself to an *earthly* crown.

Father Colley-Mahoney The ex-mistress of a king?
Mrs Thoroughfare Hush, Father! It is her constant torment! (*She sees Mrs Yajñavalkya and Niri-Esther*) Oh!
Father Colley-Mahoney The pagans are amongst us.
Mrs Thoroughfare A thimbleful of champagne ...

Mrs Thoroughfare and Father Colley-Mahoney go off

Mrs Yajñavalkya It is time for us to enter, Niri—to enter de place. (*She adjusts Niri-Esther's costume*) Princess Niri-Esther! You read dis billet-doux, my darling. It is as fraught wiv meaning as a Sultan's handkerchief.

Lady Parvula enters looking agitated

Lady Parvula Mrs Yaj!
Mrs Yajñavalkya Yes, milady?
Lady Parvula He is coming this way. Speak to him, do! I am all over nerves! (*She conceals herself behind the shrubbery*)
Mrs Yajñavalkya (*to Niri-Esther*) Run away, my child, and mingle wiv de throng. Babies are so tender ... so frail ...

Niri-Esther goes off. David enters by himself

Mrs Yajñavalkya approaches him

What do you dair so unsocial? Come on now, and hitch your wagon to a star. Up wiv dose dear shafts! You marry her—and be a lord!
David Be off! Don't pester me.
Mrs Yajñavalkya Come on now.

Lady Parvula peers out from the shrubbery

David Heart and belly, not I!

Lady Parvula is furious

Mrs Yajñavalkya Must I *pull* you?
David Don't make me a scene, because my nerves can't stand it!
Mrs Yajñavalkya Was dair ebber a eunuch like you?
David Why does she want to come bothering me?
Mrs Yajñavalkya I have nebber heard ob such contempt ob de peerage!

Lady Parvula is about to come out from hiding

David Here's Granny.

Lady Parvula withdraws again

Grannie Tooke appears, leaning on Thetis' arm

Mrs Yajñavalkya And where are you off to, Mrs Tooke?
Grannie Tooke To make a *beau-pot*, Mrs Yaj.
Mrs Yajñavalkya Wot do you call a *beau-pot*, Mrs Tooke?
Grannie Tooke A posy, Mrs Yaj.
Mrs Yajñavalkya And wot's a posy, Mrs Tooke?
Grannie Tooke A bunch of flowers, my dear.

Mrs Yajñavalkya In de East dair is a rose, deep and red, dat wen she open
go off pop, pop, pop—like de crack ob a gun!

Grannie Tooke moves off with Thetis, followed by David

Grannie Tooke Belike, Mrs Yaj. In the East, it seems, anything is possible.

The Tooke family exit

Lady Parvula emerges

Lady Parvula Insolent clodhopper!
Mrs Yajñavalkya He is frigid. But de boy is not such a fool.
Lady Parvula Marriage is not what I had in mind.
Mrs Yajñavalkya Do regard de moon, milady. Like one ob my country's
enormous grapefruit. May you enjoy ambrosia, a lover's tigerish kisses,
ere she disappears, Kra!
Lady Parvula The way things are going, that seems hardly likely. However . . .

The music recommences

> *Several couples enter. Sister Ecclesia appears, dancing on her own, and goes
> off. Sir Victor enters, and speaks to Lady Parvula who goes off with him.
> Captain Dick Thoroughfare, dark and handsome, and Lieutenant Jack
> Whorwood, young and fair, enter. They are both in naval uniform*

Nit (*seeing them*) Captain Dick!
Dick Hush, Nit! Not a word! I want to surprise my mother.
Nit As you wish, sir.

Nit exits

Dick Here we are, Jack, at Hare Hatch.
Jack It looks a fine place.
Dick Yes, and one day it will be mine—mine and Niri-Esther's.
Jack What do you think your family will say?
Dick Once they get acquainted with her, they will love her as much as I do.
Jack I hope so, Dick.
Dick I am sure of it. Oh, Jack! It's good of you to come home with me. You
have been a real chum—as Patroclus was to Achilles and even more.
Jack Thank you, Dick.

No. 17 Niri-Esther

Dick (*singing*)	You're my friend, Jack, aren't you?
Jack	Yes I am, Dick.
Dick	You'll stand by me, won't you?
Jack	Yes I will.
	And you know that I don't give a damn, Dick,
	If the world speaks well of you or ill.
Dick	We were pals together on the ocean
Jack	And on land we're comrades to the end.
	Though a sweetheart's sublime,

There is always a time
When it's fine to have a friend.

Dick (*speaking*) You will tell my mother how adorable she is, won't you?
Jack (*speaking*) I'll try.
Dick (*speaking*) Of course you will. Oh, Jack do you remember the first moment I saw her?
Jack (*speaking*) Shall I ever forget it?
Dick (*singing*)   When I first clapped eyes on Niri-Esther
She was sitting sucking melon in the sun
And I knew right then that Niri-Esther
Would be the only one.

She may be dark brown but Heaven blessed her
With the sort of charm I never hoped to see
And I found the shade of Niri-Esther
Meant not a thing to me.

Though she mayn't have social graces
And her tastes are slightly queer,
You won't find me changing places
With the noblest English peer.

For I'm more than fond of Niri-Esther
And I miss her every day that we're apart.
From the moment when I first possessed her
Niri-Esther stole my heart.

Dance chorus

Jack
Dick   Though she mayn't have social graces
          And her tastes are slightly queer,
Jack }   You won't find me changing places
Dick }   With the noblest English peer.

For I'm (he's) more than fond of Niri-Esther
And I miss (he misses) her every day that we're (they're) apart
From the moment when I (he) first possessed her
Niri-Esther stole my (his) heart.

Dick and Jack dance off. Mrs Yajñavalkya and Father Colley-Mahoney enter

Father Colley-Mahoney May I, Mrs Yaj, have the pleasure of this dance?
Mrs Yajñavalkya Why, Father Colley-Mahoney, dat would be delightful.

They begin to dance

Father Colley-Mahoney Your niece, I notice, is not dancing.
Mrs Yajñavalkya No. Just at present . . .

Father Colley-Mahoney She is not well?
Mrs Yajñavalkya Oh, she is well. But as we Eastern women say, she don't hab de inclination ...

They dance off

The music fades

> *Niri-Esther enters, sits on the swing and sings to herself. Mrs Hurstpier-point enters, sees Niri-Esther and creeps up on her*

Mrs Hurstpierpoint Is it a push you wish for, dear child? Is that what you're after?

She pushes the swing and Niri-Esther squeals

> *Mrs Thoroughfare enters and sees them*

Mrs Thoroughfare (*in agitation*) Oh! Eulalia! What are you up to?
Mrs Hurstpierpoint Go away, Thoroughfare! Now go away!
Niri-Esther Stop!

A peacock cries, off

Mrs Hurstpierpoint (*pointing*) Look! A peacock!
Niri-Esther Ours at home are much bigger.
Mrs Hurstpierpoint Are they, dear child?
Niri-Esther Much.
Mrs Hurstpierpoint I want us to be friends. Will you?
Mrs Thoroughfare Oh, Eulalia ...
Mrs Hurstpierpoint Well, Elizabeth, what is it?
Mrs Thoroughfare That girl, Eulalia; she's black!
Mrs Hurstpierpoint Black or no, she's certainly perfectly beautiful. And she was telling me, only fancy, Lizzie, that the peacocks in her land are much bigger!

> *Niri-Esther exits, unseen by Mrs Hurstpierpoint*

Mrs Thoroughfare I should think they were, Eulalia. I imagine they would be.
Mrs Hurstpierpoint I found her so interesting.
Mrs Thoroughfare I've no doubt of that, Eulalia.
Mrs Hurstpierpoint (*looking round*) But where is she?

> *The rest of the assembly begin to drift on in two's and three's; Lady Parvula appears with Sir Victor, Father Colley-Mahoney joins Mrs Hurstpierpoint, Mrs Yajñavalkya and Niri-Esther enter*

Lady Parvula ... My husband had no amorous energy whatsoever; which just suited me of course. But I—sometimes think I have too much, in spite of the ravages of time.
Sir Victor Oh, come now, Lady Parvula.
Lady Parvula But I suppose that when there's no more room for another crow's foot, one attains a sort of peace ...

Grannie Tooke and Thetis enter

Father Colley-Mahoney I forget if Sir Victor is for us or no.
Mrs Hurstpierpoint In my private list I have entered him as "Shakeable;
Very": he will come for a touch . . . (*Indicating Grannie Tooke*) She's
loose.
Father Colley-Mahoney Oh! At her time?
Mrs Hurstpierpoint Very, very loose.
Father Colley-Mahoney Indeed, she looks a limpet.
Mrs Hurstpierpoint She's shakeable, Father, I mean in other words one
could have her . . .
Mrs Yajñavalkya (*greeting Grannie Tooke*) Why, Mrs Tooke, are you still
enjoying de festivities?
Grannie Tooke So-so, Mrs Yaj. These do's a'n't what they were when I was
a girl.

The peacock is heard crying, off

Mrs Yajñavalkya Hark, Mrs Tooke, to the peacock!
Grannie Tooke Hm! A nasty sound!
Mrs Yajñavalkya Sometimes it is nasty and sometimes it is nice.
Grannie Tooke And what, Mrs Yaj, would you mean by that?

No. 19 Cry of the Peacock

Mrs Yajñavalkya
(*singing*)

When I hear de cry ob de peacock
Den I know dat something is nigh,
Maybe good, maybe bad,
But something's going to happen by and by.

When I hear de cry ob de peacock,
As it echoes ober de lawn,
Clear and shrill, something will
Be happening before tomorrow's dawn.

How I wonder if it's going to be
Something wonderful and new.
Can't you hear de peacock telling me, as he's telling
    you
Loud and true,

Dat dere's something making its way here,
Just as sure as stars in the sky,
Maybe good, maybe bad,
Maybe joyful and maybe sad,
But I know it's coming by and by
When I hear de peacock cry.

Chorus What will it be? What will it be?
Mrs Yajñavalkya All I can say is wait and see.
Chorus What will it be? What will it be?

Niri-Esther	I think it's going to happen to me!

Mrs Yajñavalkya (*speaking*) My little Niri-Esther did you hear it too?

Niri-Esther	Yes I heard de cry ob de peacock
	And I know dat something is nigh.
Mrs Yajñavalkya	It's all good, oh so good,
Niri-Esther	And it is going to happen by and by.
Mrs Yajñavalkya	When I heard de cry ob de peacock
	As it echoed ober de lawn,
Niri-Esther	Clear and shrill. Something will
	Be happening before tomorrow's dawn.
	I'm so certain dat it's going to be
	Something wonderful and new.
	Can't you hear de peacock telling me
	As he's telling you,
	Loud and true.
Chorus	Dat dere's something making its way here,
	Just as sure as stars in the sky.
	It's so good, can't be bad,
	Makes me joyful and makes me glad,
	For I know it's coming by and by
	When I hear dat peacock cry.

As the song reaches its climax, Dick enters, followed by Jack

On seeing him, Thetis utters a scream and the song stops abruptly

Thetis Oh! Is it you, Dick? Dear, is it you? Oh, Dick, Dick, Dick, my life!

Thetis attempts to fall into his arms, but Dick has eyes only for Niri-Esther. He goes to her, and they kiss passionately

Mrs Thoroughfare Dick! Dick, my darling boy!
Mrs Yajñavalkya De love-birds are reunited, Kra!
Mrs Hurstpierpoint What is she talking about?

Suddenly Niri-Esther collapses in Dick's embrace

Dick Niri! Niri-Esther, my love!
Mrs Yajñavalkya Oh, Captain Dick! Oh, Allah ilaha! You are going to be a Daddy!

Dick is overjoyed. Mrs Thoroughfare faints. Thetis has hysterics. Mrs Hurstpierpoint makes vain enquiries about what is going on. Everyone is riveted

CURTAIN

No. 20 Entr' Acte

ACT II

SCENE 1

Outside the Chapel, Hare Hatch. A sunny autumn afternoon, four or five months later

Centre-back is the chapel, very ornamental and pseudo-Gothic with double doors at present closed. There is ornamental shrubbery, a garden seat or two, and a few nude statues

When the CURTAIN *rises, Jack Whorwood is reclining on a garden seat, reading and smoking a cigarette. Upstage, Niri-Esther is posing by a statue, decorated with flowers, for Sir Victor Vatt who is at present putting finishing touches to her portrait. Niri-Esther is singing softly to herself*

Mrs Yajñavalkya wheels on a perambulator, singing a lullaby

No. 21 Little Girl Baby

Mrs Yajñavalkya   Little girl baby,
Sleep while you can.
De time is coming and it don't come slow
When you'll grow bigger and before you know
You'll be kept awake by a man.

Little girl baby,
Just you sleep on.
De time is coming in de years ahead
You'll lie uneasy on your marriage bed
Wondering where your husband has gone.

Sleep well, sleep tight,
Whether it's day or night.
Sleep sound, sleep good.
De time is coming when you'll wish you could.

Little girl baby,
Soon you'll be grown.
So sleep on now until de morning break,
De time will come when you'll be kept awake
By a little girl baby of your own.

Mrs Yajñavalkya exits at the end of the number

Sir Victor (*to Niri-Esther*) Can you turn your face a shade towards me, Miss—Mrs Thoroughfare.

Niri-Esther takes no notice and continues singing

(*To Jack*) Do you perhaps know her native tongue, sir?
Jack Yes, of course. (*To Niri-Esther*) *Ushi awabi suinya.*
Niri-Esther (*sighing*) Ah, Vishnu!
Sir Victor Not, I fear, one of my most amenable models. But then Mrs Hurstpierpoint, in her present mood, is not to be refused.
Jack Lay on the flesh tints and she won't, I dare say, be dissatisfied.

A sound of voices, off R

Oh lord, here comes the *white* Mrs Thoroughfare. (*He stands up*)

Mrs Thoroughfare enters with Dick

Mrs Thoroughfare But, my dearest boy——
Dick No, Mother, if Aunt Eulalia wishes it, then I shall fall in with her schemes. After all I am her heir. (*He goes to Sir Victor*)

Mrs Thoroughfare moves down to Jack

And how goes the portrait, Sir Victor?
Sir Victor Tolerably well, Captain. In fact it needs only a few more touches.
Niri-Esther I is tired ob standing still.
Mrs Thoroughfare Still indeed! The way she handles that Apollo.
Dick Then we shall go for a stroll, dearest Niri. (*To Sir Victor*) Forgive me, sir, but my wife is restless at the thought of our wedding tomorrow.
Sir Victor I quite understand.

Dick exits L *with Niri-Esther*

Mrs Thoroughfare But, Dick, my dear, I must talk to you . . . (*But they have gone*) Oh dear, I—oh, Sir Victor, forgive me, I almost forgot to say that ffines is serving *thé à la fourchette* in the brown drawing-room.
Sir Victor Thank you, Mrs Thoroughfare.
Mrs Thoroughfare And, Sir Victor, I have been meaning to ask you, as a surprise for Eulalia, would you paint a "Temptation of Saint Anthony"? It's a subject she has ever been fond of, it being so full of scope.
Sir Victor It would appeal to me tremendously. And for a Temptation I might perhaps ask Madame Mimosa to pose.
Mrs Thoroughfare Madame Mimosa! She doesn't seem at all a Temptation—at least, *I* shouldn't find her one.
Jack But why be dull and conventional? Why be banal?
Mrs Thoroughfare Why, what else, Lieutenant, would you suggest?
Jack Oh . . . a thousand things.
Mrs Thoroughfare But perhaps—perhaps a flower piece might be better, an arrangement, for example, of flame-coloured roses and I could tell her it's the "Burning Bush".
Sir Victor (*a little piqued*) As you wish, Mrs Thoroughfare.

Sir Victor exits

Jack takes out a comb and starts combing his hair

Mrs Thoroughfare Oh, dear, and now I've offended him. But I hardly know
what I'm saying today. Lieutenant—Lieutenant Whorwood!
Jack Oh, I'm sorry, Mrs Thoroughfare. I'm afraid I'm one of those who, at
the last Trump, would run their hand across their hair.
Mrs Thoroughfare Ah? Really—would you? Whv?
Jack Probably because I'm naturally vain.
Mrs Thoroughfare (*seeing her opening*) I adore your hair—and so does
Dick.
Jack (*surprised*) Did he say so?
Mrs Thoroughfare My boy is very fond of you.
Jack And I'm very attached to him.
Mrs Thoroughfare I know you are—and that is *why* I can talk to you about
my son.
Jack After the ceremony tomorrow, I trust you'll all at length be easy.
Mrs Thoroughfare Their re-union in my opinion is nothing but nonsense,
but Eulalia seemed so fidgety, and nervous. And with Cardinal Pirelli
come here from Spain specially to officiate. So we thought it best perhaps
to humour her.
Jack These black weddings are rarely *en règle.*
Mrs Thoroughfare I would give the whole world willingly for the poor
fellow to repudiate the affair altogether . . . But no, he's utterly infatuated
by his wife.
Jack Dear Mrs Thoroughfare, don't think I can't understand. I do . . .
absolutely.
Mrs Thoroughfare I wish I was more stoic, Lieutenant Whorwood, I wish I
had less heart . . . But I'm supersensitive. So I suffer like a fool!
Jack It isn't my business of course to meddle in souls. But Father Colley-
Mahoney should be skilled to advise.
Mrs Thoroughfare I've an inkling that Father very soon may be resigning
his post. He seems quite put out by the Cardinal.
Jack Indeed?
Mrs Thoroughfare Such a pity! None of the chaplains ever stay long . . .
They seem to resent Eulalia hauling them out of bed at night to say
Midnight Masses for her.
Jack But does she?
Mrs Thoroughfare Oh, my dear, she's merciless . . . Eulalia's inexorable . . .
Dom Jonquil, Father Ernest, she wore them *out.* You're aware of course
about the *King* . . .
Jack The old story?
Mrs Thoroughfare Her poor spirit, I fear, is everlastingly in the Royal Box
that ghastly evening of *Rigoletto.*
Jack I understand at any rate she projects presenting Mrs Richard herself
at one of the coming courts.
Mrs Thoroughfare I refuse to believe that little madcap negress was ever
born a Tahitian princess.
Jack If only she wouldn't run at one quite so much and rumple one's hair.

Mrs Thoroughfare Last night after dinner when *we* all withdrew she amused herself by smacking the hermaphrodite ...

Jack She's perhaps a little too playful.

Mrs Thoroughfare Having torn to piecemeal Eulalia's copy of *Les Chansons de Bilitis* and "mis-used" my set of dear Dumas the Elder, one might say in truth—she was destructive. And she is also very fond, I fear, of betel. Yes, I fear my boy is married to a betel-chewer.

Jack It's likely to be injurious to her baby at present.

Mrs Thoroughfare *Which?* She says she is now expecting a second *enfantement* ... Oh, she's such a quick puss.

Jack Did you discuss it with Mrs Hurst?

Mrs Thoroughfare Oh, Eulalia's so difficult. And unfortunately she isn't *mealy-mouthed* ... Eulalia says what she thinks.

As she is saying this, the chapel doors open and Mrs Hurstpierpoint appears

Mrs Hurstpierpoint Do I, Elizabeth? In what particular connection?

Mrs Thoroughfare Oh, Eulalia ... Lieutenant Whorwood and I were just discussing Niri-Esther.

Mrs Hurstpierpoint Ah, the dear minx—I thought she was sitting for Vatt's portrait.

Mrs Thoroughfare So she was, Eulalia, but darling Dick has taken her off for a stroll. She has so much excess energy.

Mrs Hurstpierpoint I would that I could borrow some of it. I have just exhausted myself going over tomorrow's ceremony with the dear Cardinal. A wedding and two christenings at one and the same time need the maximum of organization.

Cardinal Pirelli enters from the chapel. He wears a soutane and a biretta, and is a saturninely handsome old man of about seventy

Cardinal Pirelli Your chapel is even more charming than I remember it.

Mrs Hurstpierpoint Thank you, your Eminence. But it must seem a little pokey after the Cathedral.

Mrs Thoroughfare How do you like our new relics, your Eminence? I think St Automona's tooth looks a treat now that Eulalia has had it set.

Mrs Hurstpierpoint It's only a molar of course and rather small at that ...

Mrs Thoroughfare We are used lately to big flashing dentures.

Cardinal Pirelli Size isn't altogether important when one is dealing with the eternities.

Mrs Hurstpierpoint Dear Eminence, it is so good to have you with us. It will add such cachet to the whole affair.

Mrs Thoroughfare Oh, Eulalia, as if tomorrow weren't to be quite extra-ordinary as it is.

Mrs Hurstpierpoint It disturbs me, Elizabeth, that you don't get on better with your new daughter-in-law.

Mrs Thoroughfare But, Eulalia ...

Mrs Hurstpierpoint (*to Cardinal Pirelli*) She's such a fetching little piece when you get to know her, and her colour is a matter of indifference to me ...

Cardinal Pirelli That is a truly Christian attitude.

Mrs Hurstpierpoint Vatt, I notice, has painted her quite pale.
Mrs Thoroughfare Oh, if only she were!
Mrs Hurstpierpoint But she is, Elizabeth, in certain lights. She definitely is!
Mrs Thoroughfare Nonsense, Eulalia, she's as black as a sweep!
Mrs Hurstpierpoint We are boring his Eminence with all this poppycock about pigments. (*To Cardinal Pirelli*) I long to hear the news from Over There. Have you been in touch lately with Headquarters?
Cardinal Pirelli Everything in Rome appears to go on much as usual.
Mrs Hurstpierpoint I was told about Lady Laggard's audience with the Pope.
Cardinal Pirelli Ah yes, it seems she kissed his toe and then went on to do very much more ... Cynthia Laggard—such a *gamine* at one time. I remember her turning up to Midnight Mass in the Cathedral, wearing matador's rig.
Mrs Thoroughfare Did you have her turned away?
Cardinal Pirelli Certainly not! Were were all going on to the De Nazianzis' masquerade. I think I went as Sappho.
Mrs Hurstpierpoint Happy days! How I long to visit Clemenza once again!
Cardinal Pirelli Indeed you must, Mrs Hurstpierpoint. I know of no place on earth quite like it. (*He sings*)

No. 23 Cathedral of Clemenza

Clemenza!
That wonderful town.
Jack *Olé*
Cardinal Pirelli Clemenza!
Where the sun beats incessantly down
On the heavily gilded dome
Of the place that I call home.

In Paris there is Notre-Dame
And St Peter's in Rome is fine,
While St John the Divine in New York
Is indubitably divine.
I am fond of St Mark's in Venice
Tho' it's draughty when breezes blow,
But the cathedral of Clemenza
Is the cosiest church I know.

The cathedral of Barcelona
Has a beauty to quite nonplus.
I'm impressed by St Paul's in London
But it doesn't belong to us.
There's a charm to the Mosque of Omar,
Tho' one has to remove one's shoes,
But the cathedral of Clemenza
Is the church that I'd always choose.

Every transept
Is the concept
Of a truly artistic mind.
Each mosaic
Is archaic,
Individually designed.
It's rococo
Con Fuoco
With a splendour to dim the eye.

It bewitches
With its riches
And the altar's a mass
Of green Lapis Lazuli

All We must see it again before we die.
Cardinal Pirelli I have stayed at the Ritz in Paris
And my comfort was quite complete.
When I stay at the Ritz in New York
I am given the bridal suite.
I'm well known at the Ritz in London.
It's a favourite port of call.
But the cathedral of Clemenza
Is the ritziest of them all.
All Not too big, not too small,
It's the cosiest church of all.
Not too grand, not too mean,
It's the sweetest cathedral we've ever seen.
Cardinal Pirelli Clemenza!
That wonderful town
Clemenza!
Where the sun beats incessantly down
On the heavily gilded dome
Of the place that I call home.
Clemenza!

Lady Parvula enters at the end of the number

Lady Parvula (*clapping*) Olé, Eulalia! And bravo, Lieutenant!

Mrs Thoroughfare Oh, Parvula, how good to see you. You will stay for tea?

Lady Parvula No, I only looked in for a moment—to pay my respects to his Eminence.

Mrs Hurstpierpoint (*to Cardinal Pirelli*) You remember Lady Parvula de Panzoust?

Cardinal Pirelli Certainly I do.

Lady Parvula kisses his hand

Mrs Hurstpierpoint Dear Parvula is not one of us, but I think she might be won over.

Lady Parvula Not I, Eulalia. Nowadays religion of any sort is quite foreign to me. Although of course I still find a lot to enjoy in a really well staged ceremonial. Where is baby by the way?

Jack I think I see Mrs Yaj approaching!

Mrs Hurstpierpoint, Cardinal Pirelli, and Jack look off. Mrs Thoroughfare draws Lady Parvula aside

Mrs Thoroughfare (*to Lady Parvula*) Parvula, I *must* talk to you. You are my only friend.

Lady Parvula But isn't Eulalia——?

Mrs Thoroughfare Since last week Eulalia has ceased altogether to be charming.

Lady Parvula She seems in good spirits.

Mrs Thoroughfare Oh yes! But her mind—well, I shouldn't be surprised if it suddenly crashed in ruins.

Lady Parvula Of course we are none of us quite what we were . . .

Mrs Yajñavalkya can be heard, off, crooning her lullaby

Mrs Hurstpierpoint Here comes babykins!

Mrs Thoroughfare Oh, it's enough to make one's stomach capsize!

Mrs Yajñavalkya enters carrying the baby wrapped in a lace shawl

Mrs Yajñavalkya And now she is sleeping like a closed-up flower!

Mrs Hurstpierpoint (*looking at the baby*) Oh, she'll make such a cunning little Christian—almost as cunning as her mama.

Mrs Thoroughfare I can't stand it. I really can't.

Mrs Thoroughfare goes off, almost in tears

Mrs Hurstpierpoint Really, I don't know what's come over Elizabeth lately. One would have thought she would be happy to have her son again and a grandchild into the bargain. But she treats the whole thing like a second-rate Greek drama.

Mrs Yajñavalkya Maybe I should give her a sedative ob sea-weed juice. Dat always calms de nerves and settles de stomach.

Mrs Hurstpierpoint Try it, if you like, Mrs Yajñavalkya. But I would recommend a bit of prayer and mortification. I would ask Sister Ecclesia to give a helping hand, but of course it's her talking day.

Lady Parvula Was it her I heard hallooing down the drive?

Mrs Hurstpierpoint Probably. Now, Mrs Yaj, let me carry the babe for a little while. As I am to be a godmother, I had better get used to the feel of it.

Mrs Yajñavalkya (*handing the baby over*) Be careful you don't wake her, Mrs Hurst, my dear. She has a yell like de ooja bird in labour.

Mrs Hurstpierpoint Let us go to the house for tea, Eminence. I instructed Cook to prepare your favourite herring sandwiches.

Cardinal Pirelli Thank you, dear lady. And if I might have some Lapsang with a drop of Hollands in it . . .

Mrs Yajñavalkya Hollands gin for de spleen is what I always recommend.

Lady Parvula signals to Mrs Yajñavalkya

Mrs Hurstpierpoint And you, Parvula?

Lady Parvula No, thank you, Eulalia. I have ordered *à la carte* at the *Strangers'*, and their dinner hours are barbarous.

Mrs Hurstpierpoint Well, we shall see you tomorrow at the ceremony. Lieutenant?

Jack I think I'll take a stroll after Dick and Niri. I've seen so little of the Valmouth countryside.

Mrs Hurstpierpoint Oh, you should. The autumn tints on Spadder Tor are supposed to be quite heartrending. Come, Eminence.

Mrs Hurstpierpoint and the Cardinal go off R. *Jack goes off* L

Lady Parvula Oh, thank goodness we are alone. It was of course you whom I came to see. I'm making my final bid.

Mrs Yajñavalkya Final, milady?

Lady Parvula Yes—although I fear he must be cold, or else he's decadent, for I have known men, Mrs Yajñavalkya—yes and *many men* too!—who have found us little women the most engrossing things in life——

Mrs Yajñavalkya He is inhuman, milady, and dat is sure.

Lady Parvula Oh ... I want to spank the white walls of his cottage!

Mrs Yajñavalkya I obtain you all you desire: only give me time.

Lady Parvula I have no more time to spare. The Valmouth season is practically over, and I shall have to return to London—*unfulfilled*!

Mrs Yajñavalkya I could get you de pageboy from de *Strangers' Hotel*.

Lady Parvula Too young!

Mrs Yajñavalkya He twelve.

Lady Parvula Go on! He's not eight.

Mrs Yajñavalkya Dat child is a king's morsel!

Lady Parvula (*shaking her head*) In the depths of the wilds you'd think young folk were bound to be more or less pent up.

Mrs Yajñavalkya It is not right, my dear, you should be bilked ... What do you say to de Captain ob a ketch?

Lady Parvula As a rule that class is much too Esau, you understand what I mean?

Mrs Yajñavalkya Or have you ever looked attentively at de local schoolmaster?

Lady Parvula Schoolmaster? No! I have set my mind on this wretched shepherd.

Mrs Yajñavalkya Well, what do you wish me to do?

Lady Parvula I overheard his grandmother sending him up here with some fowls for tomorrow's banquet. He will be arriving any moment. Go down to the gate and tell him to walk up this way. And I shall be waiting!

Mrs Yajñavalkya Very well, milady, and may Phoona smile on you.

Lady Parvula Phoona?

Mrs Yajñavalkya Dat is how we Eastern ladies refer to Venus!

Mrs Yajñavalkya goes off L

Lady Parvula (*to herself*) I know I should despise myself, but I don't! Such perfect cant, though, with four honeymoons in the hotel, to be forced to take to the fields . . . (*She sings*)

No. 24 Only A Passing Phase

Oh Haree, oh Haree,
Are you gazing down from Heaven on little me?
And are you simply horrified by what you see?
Please don't be, dear Haree.
For you left your little wifey
All alone to lead her lifey,
And she's doing it the only way she knows.
I may be a wayward creature,
But I've one redeeming feature.
Would you like me to explain to you? Here goes . . .

There was the gardener at the Towers
And he had a way with me as well as flowers.
But it was only a passing phase.
Because I lighted on his brother
Who had come to do some plumbing job or other.
But it was only a passing phase.

For at the weekend I went shooting
And it broke the plumber's spell,
Because I bagged a brace of pheasant
And a beater as well.

But then he beat me where it hurt me,
And I felt my ardour suddenly desert me,
So I remained completely chaste for several days.
But it was only a passing phase.

One of our footmen, as they oft do,
Looked so handsome with his livery on, and off too.
But it was only a passing phase.

Because the chauffeur, so endearing,
Drove me far, but had some trouble with his steering,
So that was only a passing phase.

And to forget him I went yachting,
And the trip I just adored,
For though I spent the time between decks,
I went right overboard.

But sailors can be rather wearing,
And the stoker, I recall, was quite unsparing.
So I resolved to take the veil and change my ways.

But it was only a
Very transitory, evanescent,
Insubstantial, quite unpleasant,
Passing phase.
It's over now.

David enters at the end of the number. He is carrying some dead chickens

David (*seeing Lady Parvula*) Oh! It's you, is it?
Lady Parvula Yes, it is I. Don't they say good-afternoon in this part of the
country?
David Good-afternoon. (*He moves off*)
Lady Parvula Don't go! Won't you tell me about—your *flocks*?
David I have to deliver these fowls at the house.
Lady Parvula They can wait surely. After all, they are dead. (*Advancing
towards him*) Whereas we, dear fellow, are very much alive ...
David Now, don't 'ee come near me.
Lady Parvula Why? Do you have the flu?
David You know what I mean. I told Mrs Yaj. I didn't want no part of 'ee.
Lady Parvula I know you did, and it was very forward of you.
David There's forward and forward ...
Lady Parvula Meaning what?
David You should be a respectable widder-woman.
Lady Parvula Instead of which I am ...?
David I dunno what 'ee are.
Lady Parvula Why don't you find out? It might be quite an agreeable
surprise.
David I've enough to do without being surprised.
Lady Parvula Bah! Country logic!
David Well, if this is how they behave London way——
Lady Parvula (*making a dive at him*) Oh, you great big pastoral boy!
David (*warding her off with the fowls*) Now then, missus!
Lady Parvula Oh, you might at least lay aside the carcasses. They do detract
so from the ardour of the moment.
David Why don't 'ee leave me be?
Lady Parvula (*advancing on him again*) Because I don't wish to. Ah those
great gilt freckles!
David I'll roar for help!
Lady Parvula Much better submit!
David I won't, I say.
Lady Parvula I say you will!

She attempts to embrace him. Voices are heard, off

David Someone's coming!
Lady Parvula Damnation! (*Looking round her*) Quick, into the chapel
before they see us!
David But ...
Lady Parvula In, I say!

She drags him into the chapel, protesting. Mrs Thoroughfare and Father Colley-Mahoney enter

Mrs Thoroughfare I thought I saw some struggling figures . . . But there seems to be no-one . . . I'm sorry, Father, you were saying?

Father Colley-Mahoney That you must have faith, my child. All may not be lost.

Mrs Thoroughfare But tomorrow is nearly upon us. And Eulalia is quite determined. She has arranged everything down to the last altar-candle. What can interfere with it now?

Father Colley-Mahoney Without a priest . . .

Mrs Thoroughfare But she has the Cardinal. I must say I thought his Eminence would raise some objection, but he seems to be enjoying the whole *saturnalia* himself.

Father Colley-Mahoney Cardinal Pirelli has strange tendencies.

Mrs Thoroughfare Tendencies, Father?

Father Colley-Mahoney There are rumours, strong rumours, from Clemenza. Reports, even from Rome.

Mrs Thoroughfare Reports? Of what?

Father Colley-Mahoney Ecclesiastical misdemeanours . . . Extramural escapades . . . and the disgraceful affair of the Duquesa de Nazianzi's dog . . .

Mrs Thoroughfare What did the dog do?

Father Colley-Mahoney It was christened—in the Cathedral.

Mrs Thoroughfare (*horror-struck*) Father!

Father Colley-Mahoney Christened Clapsy—by the Cardinal.

Mrs Thoroughfare But—but this means . . .

Father Colley-Mahoney Yes, my child. But at the moment I am powerless.

Mrs Thoroughfare Oh, we must do something! We *must* do something! Oh, my darling Dick! Oh . . . oh!

Father Colley-Mahoney Calm yourself, Mrs Thoroughfare. Let us go into the chapel and pray for guidance.

Mrs Thoroughfare Oh yes, let us. (*She goes to the chapel door and opens it. Shrieking*) Oh-h-h!

Father Colley-Mahoney What is it?

Mrs Thoroughfare Sacrilege . . .! Blasphemy . . .! Chickens, Father . . . Chickens . . .!

Father Colley-Mahoney Chickens?

Mrs Thoroughfare Yes . . . in the font . . . And . . . oh-h-h!

She faints in Father Colley-Mahoney's arms

David emerges from the chapel looking very shaken. He touches his forelock to Father Colley-Mahoney and makes off L. After a moment or two Lady Parvula comes out. She is covered in chicken-feathers

Father Colley-Mahoney Lady de Panzoust!

Mrs Thoroughfare (*reviving*) Parvula!

Lady Parvula Tell Eulalia—tell Eulalia that her pew-cushions badly need re-stuffing.

Lady Parvula musters her dignity and walks off L

Mrs Thoroughfare faints again. The Lights fade, quickly

SCENE 2

The Banks of the River Val. Immediately following

David and Niri-Esther enter

No. 25 Valmouth (Reprise)

Dick (*singing*)   There's no air
To compare with the air
Of Valmouth.
There's no light
That's as bright as the light
Of Valmouth.
On the banks of the Val.
Circled by the friendly hills
Sheltered by the sky,
Safe are we from wordly ills
Time that kills
Passes us by.
In Valmouth
Every care
Seems to fade in the air
Of Valmouth
There's a balm
To be found in the calm
Of Valmouth, on the banks of the Val.
Come and spend a while with us
And learn to sigh and smile with us.
And when you leave it,
Strange as it seems,
Valmouth stays in your dreams.

Niri-Esther attempts to kiss Dick

(*Speaking*) No, Niri! Not now.
Niri-Esther Why not!
Dick Because—because it's tea-time.
Niri-Esther In de East we don't care what time it is.
Dick I know, but this is England. And anyway someone might observe us.
Niri-Esther I like love out ob doors. Dat big old bed at Hare Hatch frightens me.
Dick Don't say that, my darling. Hare Hatch is our home.
Niri-Esther No.
Dick But——
Niri-Esther I is tired ob Hare Hatch. I is tired ob Valmouth.

Dick But don't you find it beautiful? Look at the river, flowing out to sea.
Look at the hills, look at the autumn leaves on the trees——

Niri-Esther De leaves are turning brown. Dat makes me sad.

Dick But they'll be green again next spring. Don't you like Valmouth in the
Spring?

Niri-Esther (*shouting*) I is tired ob de Valmouth air! I is tired ob de
Valmouth light! And I is sick to death ob religion!

Dick Niri!

Niri-Esther I want de sun, de joy, de heat! (*She sings*)

No. 26 Where The Trees Are Green With Parrots

Where de trees are green with parrots
And de custard apples grow,
Dat is de place dat I call home,
Dat's where I want to go.

Where de golden toad sits dreaming
Underneath de orchid tree,
Dat is de place dat I call home,
Dat's where I want to be.

Where de scent ob de frangi-pani
Floats to sea where de breezes blow
And at night dere's de plop
As de mangoes drop
From de branches where de fire-flies glow.

Where de coral spreads its flowers
In a sea dat's greeny blue,
Dat is de place dat I call home,
Dere's where I want to be with you.

(*Speaking*) Say we go there! Say we will go home!

Dick Well—perhaps, if you are a good girl, one day ... But we must go
through with the ceremony tomorrow. My aunt expects it.

Niri-Esther But we is already married!

Dick Not in the eyes of the Church. Please, Niri, for my sake ...

Niri-Esther Oh, all right. But I do it for you, not for dat old Cardinal!

*She flounces off and Dick follows her. As they go Thetis enters. She has
obviously been following them. She looks even more woebegone than before,
her hair in disorder and her clothes uncared for*

Thetis I love you, Dick—I asked for nothing better, dear, than to be the
wool of your vest ... I'd have blacked myself for you, Dick. All over every
day. But you never told me your tastes ...! But everything's useless now.
For very soon, Dick. I'll be dead! (*She steps on to the bank*)

Carry (*off, calling*) Miss Thetis! Miss Thetis!

Thetis steps down again, looking irritated

Carry enters, carrying a bunch of flowers

I've followed 'ee all the way from town. But 'ee walked so fast!

Thetis What do you want, Carry Smith?

Carry Just to talk to 'ee, Miss Thetis. Oh, Miss! I know at last ...

Thetis What do you know?

Carry I know *at last*—about the gentlemen.

Thetis About what gentlemen?

Carry I know all about them.

Thetis So do I—traitors.

Carry Oh, miss! They're not!

Thetis Don't be a fool, Carry Smith.

Carry But I *know*!

Thetis You may think you do. But you wait until you're my age. Look what happened to me ... (*She sings*)

> I loved a man and he sailed away
> Ah hé, ah hé.
> He sailed away on the ocean main
> And here I wait till he comes again
> Ah hé, ah hé, ah hé.

(*Speaking*) And now leave me alone, Carry.

Carry But, miss——

Thetis Go home. And remember what I told you.

Carry is silenced by the tone of her voice and moves off slowly, finally running

Thetis moves on to the bank, she looks down into the water

It's so cold now, and so deep. I suppose the tide will bear me out to sea. I'm so lightsome, so slim—a much better figure than *hers*.

She is about to jump, when Sister Ecclesia is heard, off, shouting a stream of words

Sister Ecclesia enters still shouting

Sister Ecclesia Brown bread and butter, outhouse, silk stockings, Gorgonzola, arpeggio, flat-feet, verandah, self-importance, long yellow hair, three weeks next Wednesday, one and one make ninety-seven, bag and baggage, harpsichords, Mrs Hurst's hats, paraphernalia, catastrophe, appendicitis, encyclopedia!

Thetis sees her, and turns away. She is about to leap when Sister Ecclesia notices her

Stop! Halt! Cease! Desist!

Thetis I won't! Go away!

She is about to jump, but Sister Ecclesia runs up to her and grabs her

Sister Ecclesia Wicked, ghastly, tragic, illegal, fatal, monstrous, lamentable——

Thetis Leave me be!

They struggle

Sister Ecclesia You mustn't, you shan't, you won't, you can't——
Thetis I can and I will!
Sister Ecclesia (*hanging on to her*) Help, aid, assistance, succour!

Jack enters, running

Jack What's the matter?
Sister Ecclesia She wants to kill herself!
Thetis Yes, I do! And I'm going to!
Sister Ecclesia But it's so wonderful to be alive, exist, breathe——
Thetis Aren't you supposed to be under a vow of silence?
Sister Ecclesia Yes! But today—is my talking day! (*She sings*)

No. 27 My Talking Day

I can speak, I can utter,
I can scream, I can mutter,
I can say everything I want to say
And there's no-one to say me nay,
For today is my talking day.

I can rant, I can chatter,
I can shriek, what's it matter?
I can bark, I can bellow, I can bay.
Not a soul has to say I may,
For today is my talking day.

Words, words, words, words,
Waiting for me to speak
Words, words, words, words,
How I wish I knew Greek!

I can bawl, I can babble,
I can gush, I can gabble,
I can moo, I can yodel, I can neigh.
Tomorrow my lips will be sealed again,
My heart will be cold and congealed again,
But till then raise the roof and shout hurray,
For today is my talking day.

I can yell, I can yammer,
I can sing, I can stammer,
I can squawk, I can chirrup, I can bray,
And I'll do so without delay,
For today is my talking day.

I can joke, I can jabber,
I can belch, I can blabber,
I can preach, I can prattle, I can pray

Till the sun sheds its dying ray,
For today is my talking day.

Words, words, words, words,
Echoing through the air.
Words, words, words, words,
And I might even swear.

I can groan, I can grumble,
I can mew, I can mumble,
I can make any sound you care to say.
Tomorrow my lips will be dumb again,
My heart will be silent and numb again,
But till then raise the roof and shout hurray,
For today is my talking day.
    (*Speaking*) So you see, there's always something to live for.
Jack She is right, you know.
Sister Ecclesia Take her away, Lieutenant. She's young, beautiful, fresh,
    pretty, desirable, virginal——
Thetis I'm not!
Sister Ecclesia High-spirited, amorous, adorable——
Jack Come, Miss Tooke. I'll take you home.
Thetis Oh, very well. But, I'll do it tomorrow instead—you wait.
Jack Tomorrow is the wedding. Why don't you come with me?
Thetis (*appraising him*) With you? Well . . .
Jack Shall we go?

Jack takes Thetis off

Sister Ecclesia Love, passion, courtship, wooing, darling, sweetheart . . .
    (*She sings*)

No. 27A. My Talking Day (Reprise)

I can speak, I can utter,
I can scream, I can mutter,
I can say everything I want to say
And there's no-one to say me nay,
For today is my talking day.

Fade to Black-out

SCENE 3

Outside the Chapel, Hare Hatch. The next day

*A canopy has been set up over the entrance to the chapel, and the doors are
flung open*

ffines is supervising the final arrangements. He gives instructions to Nit, the footman, and Fowler, as they run back and forth from the chapel, with flowers, prayer-books, plates of sandwiches, etc. Finally, everything is ready and he marshals them off

Mrs Yajñavalkya enters, resplendent in her best clothes

Mrs Yajñavalkya (*ecstatically*) Dis is de day, de day dat my little Niri, my Princess, my Niri-fairy becomes Mrs Captain Dick Thoroughfare! Oh, Allah ilaha!

Granny Tooke enters, wearing her best bonnet and leaning on a stick

Granny Tooke Is that you, Mrs Yaj?

Mrs Yajñavalkya Why, Mrs Tooke, have you come to attend de wedding?

Granny Tooke Yes, Mrs Yaj. You heard, I suppose, about my granddaughter?

Mrs Yajñavalkya Your granddaughter, Mrs Tooke? You mean her attempted *felo-de-se*?

Granny Tooke I don't know what you choose to call it. All I know is that the sea would have absorbed her if that silent sister hadn't intervened.

Mrs Yajñavalkya Dat is nothing but Kismet, Mrs Tooke.

Granny Tooke Whatever it is, it's nearly turned her mind. And all because the Captain's marrying your niece, Mrs Yaj. What will happen to Hare Hatch with a savage for a mistress?

Mrs Yajñavalkya It will be better, Mrs Tooke. Niri-Esther say dat de first improvement she make will be to flatten de roof.

Granny Tooke Well, at least she's having a Christian wedding.

Mrs Yajñavalkya Dat is just to please Mrs Hurst. Dey are already married in de East.

Granny Tooke Pah! A native wedding!

Mrs Yajñavalkya It is so simple, so beautiful! All dat happen is dat each lays a hand on de torso of de beloved.

Granny Tooke Fie, Mrs Yaj, for shame.

Mrs Yajñavalkya But what need is dere for more? Oh, dear, it shock me dat Niri should renounce Allah for de Nazarene.

Granny Tooke (*shocked*) As I'm a decent widow, Mrs Yaj, you are a wicked woman.

Mrs Yajñavalkya Me wicked? Now dat is a libel!

Granny Tooke Libel or not, things haven't been the same since you came to Valmouth.

Mrs Yajñavalkya Don't fret yourself, Mrs Tooke. Once I see my Niri settled at Hare I shall leave dis place. Valmouth is beginning to give me de *ennui*.

Granny Tooke You'll be going back home?

Mrs Yajñavalkya I don't know. I shall just sail away, down de river.

Granny Tooke Down the river? Well, though I shouldn't say so, I'll miss you, Mrs Yaj. With the winter coming my joints will be tied up in knots. I doubt if I'll see another spring.

Mrs Yajñavalkya Why, Mrs Tooke, my dear, you talk nothing but nonsense.

No. 28 I Will Miss You

Granny Tooke (*singing*) **Mrs Yajñavalkya**	I never came to see Your blossoming acacia tree. It's leaves are falling now as summer ends. But nevertheless we have some gay times.
Granny Tooke	Oh, yes Mrs Yaj, it's true we did.
Mrs Yajñavalkya	And taking it all in all I'd like to feel we're friends. And when I think of Valmouth, I won't miss these skies of grey Dat seem to happen every day: I like a sky dat's permanently blue. But I will miss you, Mrs Tooke Yes I will, Mrs Tooke, miss you.

And I won't miss de frightful bore
Of English Sundays, and what's more
I'll never miss de foggy foggy dew.
But I will miss you, Mrs Tooke,
Yes I will, Mrs Tooke, miss you.

Although we had our quarrels
Dey mattered not a pin.
We may have different morals
But we're sisters under the skin.

And when I'm on dat tropic isle
As evening falls I'll sit and smile
And think of all dat's passed between us two.
And I will miss you, Mrs Tooke.

Granny Tooke	And I will, Mrs Yaj, miss you.
Mrs Yajñavalkya	And I will miss you, Mrs Tooke.
Both	I will miss you.
Granny Tooke	Life will go on much the same As life went on before you came. I'll do the things I always used to do. But I will miss you, Mrs Yaj. Yes I will, Mrs Yaj, miss you.

And though we're friends, I must confess
I can't abide the way you dress.
Those heathen things you say upset me too.
But I will miss you, Mrs Yaj.
Yes I will, Mrs Yaj, miss you.

You turned us topsy-turvy
With all those things you've done.
It's left me rather nervy
But I must admit it was fun.

And when the winter brings the snow
I'll sit and watch the cinders glow
And think of all that's passed between us two
And I will miss you, Mrs Yaj.
Mrs Yajñavalkya And I will, Mrs Tooke, miss you
Granny Tooke And I will miss you, Mrs Yaj.
Both I will miss you.
We must keep in touch.

ffines appears at the end of the number and takes up his station outside the chapel to usher in the wedding guests, one or two of whom come on and stand around chatting. Mrs Thoroughfare enters in a state

Mrs Thoroughfare Oh there you are, Mrs Yajñavalkya! Your niece has been calling for you to help her dress. She refuses to let Fowler touch her.
Mrs Yajñavalkya Oh, she is unaccustomed to clothes, Mrs Thoroughfare, my dear.
Mrs Thoroughfare I can well believe it.
Mrs Yajñavalkya Why, in de East until de age ob nineteen we nebber have more in de course ob a year dan a bit ob cotton loincloth. You may wear it how you please, my poor mother would say, but dat is all you'll get! And so, dear me, I generally used to put it on my head!

Mrs Yajñavalkya goes off chortling

Mrs Thoroughfare greets the guests

Mrs Thoroughfare (*to Grannie Tooke*) How good of you to come, Mrs Tooke—under the circumstances, I mean. Has your granddaughter quite recovered?
Granny Tooke Oh, she's a brawny girl, and in any case she barely wet her toes.

Sir Victor enters with Lady Saunter

Mrs Thoroughfare (*going to them*) Sir Victor and Lady Saunter! How nice to see you! At a time like this one needs one's friends around one.
Lady Saunter Oh you can be sure that we wouldn't miss it for worlds.
Mrs Thoroughfare I can't think what is delaying Eulalia.
Sir Victor Should we go into the chapel? It looks as if it might rain.
Mrs Thoroughfare Oh dear, a storm, do you think? The wrath of the Almighty?

Mrs Hurstpierpoint enters carrying the baby in a long christening robe. She is wearing an elaborate gown with beaded wings at her shoulders, and on her face is a black mask

Mrs Thoroughfare is aghast

Mrs Hurstpierpoint Tell me. Elizabeth, will I do?
Mrs Thoroughfare *Do*! Eulalia—I never saw anything like you.
Mrs Hurstpierpoint I hope the dear Cardinal won't tell me I'm unorthodox or do you think he will?
Mrs Thoroughfare Take it off, Eulalia.

Mrs Hurstpierpoint I shall not, Elizabeth!

Mrs Thoroughfare Take it off!

Mrs Hurstpierpoint No!

Mrs Thoroughfare But why should you conceal yourself behind that odious mask?

Mrs Hurstpierpoint I wear it, dear, only because a white face seems to frighten baby.

Mrs Thoroughfare You're beyond anything, Eulalia.

Dick and Jack, both in full-dress uniform, enter and talk to the guests

Mrs Hurstpierpoint Ah, dear Richard! Let us hope the bride will soon join us. And we mustn't keep her standing about. There's quite a chill in the air . . .

Mrs Thoroughfare And those clouds . . .

Mrs Hurstpierpoint I had such a cold on *my* honeymoon, I remember, I never really ceased sneezing.

Lady Parvula enters in a "light, décolleté day-dress" and a "white beret de Picador"

Oh, there's dear Parvula, looking ravishing, as usual.

Mrs Thoroughfare I shan't speak to her, Eulalia.

Mrs Hurstpierpoint Why ever not, Eliza?

Mrs Thoroughfare I prefer not to say.

Mrs Hurstpierpoint Oh, very well. (*Going to Lady Parvula*) Parvula, you look delightful!

Lady Parvula Eulalia, it's you, is it? I confess that I hardly recognized you . . .

Mrs Hurstpierpoint That hat is a triumph. Where did you get it, Parvula!

Lady Parvula Vivi Vanderstart. Her boast is, she makes only "Hats for Happy Women" . . .

They talk, Mrs Thoroughfare moves to Sir Victor

Mrs Thoroughfare Dear Sir Victor, couldn't you persuade my friend to doff that mask?

Sir Victor If you, Mrs Thoroughfare, can't, I hardly think that I——

Mrs Thoroughfare We have always been so close. Eulalia and I arranged that whichever of us dies first will keep a place for the other in Paradise: and if there isn't room for two, we'll just sit on each other's knees. But now I fear——

Sir Victor It is sad, isn't it, how the old Hare days seem completely gone: vanished.

Mrs Thoroughfare One can hardly expect people to visit here now, Niri-Esther is so eccentric!

They move upstage. Mrs Hurstpierpoint moves down with Lady Parvula

David enters with Thetis, who has dressed herself up and wears a big hat

Lady Parvula Will you take the bride to London for the season?

Mrs Hurstpierpoint I hope to. She loves lights and commotion, which goes to show she has social instincts.

Lady Parvula Well, it's some time I suppose since there's been a negress . . .
Mrs Hurstpierpoint She should be an instant success.
Lady Parvula All the fair men, the blondes, she will take from us . . .
Mrs Hurstpierpoint You, my dear, have nothing to fear.
Lady Parvula Somehow, now it doesn't seem to matter. I feel perhaps I
have really had my final fling . . .

*David finds himself beside her as she says this and turns away in confusion.
There is a sudden hush, and a peacock is heard calling*

Mrs Hurstpierpoint Listen to that! When the peacocks cry, I always get a
feeling of foreboding.

There is the sound of organ music

   Mrs Yajñavalkya runs on excitedly

Mrs Thoroughfare (*running to Mrs Hurstpierpoint*) Oh, Eulalia, Eulalia, I
appeal to you! Let us drop the ceremony now, before it's too late!
Mrs Hurstpierpoint Nonsense, Elizabeth!
Mrs Thoroughfare Oh, if only I knew where to find Father Colley!
Mrs Hurstpierpoint Hush, Elizabeth.
Mrs Yajñavalkya Oh Allah ilaha! The bride, she approaches!

   *Sister Ecclesia enters carrying a religious banner, followed by Nit, in a
   surplice, swinging an incense-burner. Finally, Cardinal Pirelli appears in full
   regalia*

*The Cardinal stands C in-front of the chapel door. On his left are Dick and
Jack and Mrs Hurstpierpoint with the baby. The others range themselves on
either side in preparation for the entry into chapel*

   *As Pinpipi's voice rings out ·from the chapel, Niri-Esther enters in bridal
   attire; her train is held by Carry Smith*

There are gasps of admiration and Mrs Hurstpierpoint is ecstatic

Pinpipi   "Grant, O grant, that she shall find,
   (*off, singing*)   On Yniswitrins's altars pale,
                         The vision of the Holy Grail."
Mrs Hurstpierpoint *Ah, les oiseaux amoureux, chers oiseaux* . . . paradise
uccellinis . . . delicious *vogels* . . .
Mrs Thoroughfare (*in tears*) Oh my darling son!
Dick Hush, Mother!

Pinpipi's voice rises to a climax as the Cardinal turns to enter the chapel

   *Suddenly Father Colley-Mahoney rushes on brandishing a parchment with a
   seal*

Father Colley-Mahoney Stop!

*Everyone stops in their tracks. The music ceases and Pinpipi's voice trails into
silence*

Mrs Hurstpierpoint Father Colley! Have you taken leave of your senses?

Father Colley-Mahoney The wedding cannot proceed!
Mrs Thoroughfare Glory be to God!
Mrs Hurstpierpoint (*to Father Colley-Mahoney*) Of course the wedding can
proceed! (*To Cardinal Pirelli*) Forgive us, Eminence——
Father Colley-Mahoney If he sets foot inside Nuestra Señora it will be
desecrated for ever!
Mrs Hurstpierpoint (*shrieking*) What!

*Everyone begins anxiously whispering to each other. Dick puts his arm round
Niri-Esther*

Father Colley-Mahoney (*brandishing the parchment*) I have here in my hand
a Deed of Excommunication signed by the Holy Father in Rome.
Cardinal Pirelli, your sins have found you out! You are excommunicated!

A gasp of horror goes up from the assembly

Mrs Hurstpierpoint It can't be true! It can't be! Eminence . . .

But the Cardinal has sunk to his knees, and is mumbling prayers

Father Colley-Mahoney (*reading*) "For the sin of blasphemy, for the sin of
impurity, for the sin of mockery, for the sin of dressing up in disguise, for
the sin of reading and writing sacrilegious literature, for the sin of
christening a dog, the Holy Church casts you out."
Mrs Thoroughfare It is the wrath of the Almighty!
Mrs Yajñavalkya Oh Allah ilaha! Oh Kismet!

*Niri-Esther tears off her veil, runs to Mrs Hurstpierpoint snatches the baby
from her and runs off*

Dick Niri! Niri-Esther! Come back.
Mrs Yajñavalkya She is flying, Captain Dick! She is flying away like a little
white bird!

Dick runs off in pursuit

Mrs Thoroughfare Dick! Dick! My darling boy!
Thetis (*screaming*) Dick! Now you can come back to me!

Violent thunder

Lady Parvula Heavens, what a débâcle!

A crash of thunder and the sound of torrential rain

ffines The river! The river is rising!
Nit The river is rising!

Panic breaks out as the Lights fade

SCENE 4

The Valmouth Road, Immediately following

The storm noises continue until the Lights come up

Niri-Esther runs across the stage. Dick is heard off, calling her

Dick (*off*) Niri! Niri-Esther! Come back!

Dick enters

Niri-Esther! Where are you?

Mrs Thoroughfare enters

Mrs Thoroughfare Dick! Come back. Come back to Hare!
Dick But I must find her!
Mrs Thoroughfare It's the best thing, my darling Dick. It was never right . . .
Dick Let me go, Mother. I must find her.

Dick runs off

Mrs Thoroughfare Dick! Dick!

Sir Victor, Lady Saunter and Lady Parvula enter

Sir Victor Mrs Thoroughfare! You must take shelter.
Mrs Thoroughfare But, Dick——
Lady Parvula As far as I can see, it's everyone for himself.
Lady Saunter If only we could find a cab.
Lady Parvula All I want is the first train to London.
Sir Victor We must hurry! Hurry!

Grannie Tooke enters supported by David. Sir Victor and Lady Saunter go off

Granny Tooke It's the end of us all. It's the end of everything.
Lady Parvula Oh, don't say that, Mrs Tooke. Valmouth isn't the only place on earth.
Granny Tooke It is to me!
Lady Parvula (*to David*) Why don't you come to London? You could be my chauffeur.
David I'm a shepherd.
Lady Parvula Oh, bother your sheep!
David (*ignoring her*) Come, Granny. We must get home!

David takes Grannie Tooke off

Lady Parvula Well, that's that! But at least it livened up my holiday!

Thetis, Sister Ecclesia and Jack enter

Jack Go back to the house, Mrs Thoroughfare.
Lady Parvula Come, Elizabeth—back to Hare. Eulalia is all alone.

A loud clap of thunder

Mrs Thoroughfare Merciful heavens! It's like Doomsday.
Lady Parvula I'm much afraid, Elizabeth, that time has caught up with us at last.

A flash of lightning and a crash. Sister Ecclesia raises her hand and points, mouthing frantically

Mrs Thoroughfare (*moaning*) O-o-oh!
Lady Parvula (*looking off*) It's Hare! Hare has been struck by lightning.
Mrs Thoroughfare Eulalia! My dear friend!

The thunder increases in volume as the Lights fade

SCENE 5

Tarooa. Some months later

The Lights come up on Niri-Esther, seated on the ground nursing her new baby. Beside her is the perambulator

No. 31 Where The Trees Are Green With Parrots (Reprise)

Niri-Esther   Where de coral spreads its flowers
(*singing*)   In a sea dat's greeny-blue.
              Dat is de place dat I call home,
              Dere's where I want to be with you.

Mrs Yajñavalkya bustles in, wearing a sarong and carrying her doctor's bag

Mrs Yajñavalkya Oh deary me, de troubles dat Mrs Bjopti suffers from her embonpoint! (*Seeing Niri-Esther*) Why, Niri-Esther has been crying again? (*She runs to her*)
Niri-Esther I cry a little for Richard—little Richard with no papa.
Mrs Yajñavalkya Children without a papa on this island are quite commonplace, my dear. However, I shall find you a new husband.

Niri-Esther brightens

Soon dere will come another ship into the harbour. And this time, little Niri, perhaps you will find an admiral!
Niri-Esther An admiral?
Mrs Yajñavalkya Yes. And den you will go and live in a fine house in London. Kra!
Niri-Esther But I wanted to be de princess of de palace, de palace of Hare Hatch.
Mrs Yajñavalkya Hare Hatch? Hare Hatch is nothing but a pile of ashes. Allah sent de fire from Heaven and destroyed it—pouf!—in a flash of lightning.
Niri-Esther Den we shall nebber see it again?
Mrs Yajñavalkya No, my child, it is all gone. And Valmouth too—gone like a dream. It was de will ob Allah.
Niri-Esther But I shall remember it.
Mrs Yajñavalkya Yes, and I shall remember it too. It was a pleasant place to spend a season, or as we Eastern ladies say, to pass de time.

No. 32 Finale

As the music of "Valmouth" starts softly, the Lights begin to fade

Niri-Esther Little Richard sleep.
Mrs Yajñavalkya (*abstractedly*) Sleep good, little boy baby sleep tight. Yes, it is all gone. Sometimes I think "Oh de pity ob it". In Valmouth I had such an extensive clientele—all de best ladies ob de county. "Mrs Yaj," dey would say to me, "you must have magic in your fingers." "Yes, my dear," I would reply, "dat is exactly what I do have." Oh, dey will miss me, dose old ladies ob Valmouth. Dey will miss deir Mrs Yaj. But perhaps dey are dead, or perhaps dey are living somewhere else. Who knows? Still I would like to take a trip to England some time, when I have found you a new husband.
Niri-Esther Where would you go?
Mrs Yajñavalkya Oh, I don't know. Bournemouth is nice.
Madame Mimosa (*off, singing*) Valmouth!
Mrs Yajñavalkya And den dere is Weymouth.
Fowler (*off, singing*)   Valmouth!
Mrs Yajñavalkya Or Exmouth.
Dr Dee (*off, singing*)   Valmouth!
Mrs Yajñavalkya Or even Portsmouth.
Dick (*off, singing*)   Valmouth!
Mrs Yajñavalkya But none ob dem can ever compare wiv Valmouth.
All (*off, singing*)   Valmouth!
Dick (*off*) Come back, Niri-Esther, come back!
Jack (*off*) If only she wouldn't run at one so much and rumple one's hair . . .
Thetis (*off*) I'm so lightsome, so slim, a much better figure than hers . . .
David (*off*) 'Od! You're a simple one, you are! . . .
Lady Parvula (*off*) Why, Elizabeth, tonight you look positively *jeune fille* . . .
Mrs Thoroughfare (*off*) I always say that there is no joy like the coolness of a white dress after the sweetness of confession . . .
Father Colley-Mahoney (*off*) Fie, Thoroughfare . . .!
Cardinal Pirelli (*off*) Size is not altogether important when one is dealing with the eternities . . .
Granny Tooke (*off*) I'm making a *beau-pot*, that's a posy, Mrs Yaj . . .
Mrs Hurstpierpoint (*off*) Blunt-headed booby! To Valmouth, by way of Fleet . . .
All (*off, singing*)   Valmouth!

As the song ends, the Lights fade to a spot on Mrs Yajñavalkya, and she is on the verge of tears

CURTAIN

FURNITURE AND PROPERTY LIST

Only essential items are listed. Further dressing may be added at the director's discretion.

ACT I

SCENE 1

On stage: Carriage

Personal: **Mrs Hurstpierpoint:** parasol
Father Colley-Mahoney: prayer-book

SCENE 2

On stage: Daleman statue
Chair, easel, painting, paints, brushes etc. (for **Sir Victor**)

Off stage: Chair **(Thetis)**
Wreath **(Dr Dee)**

Personal: **Mrs Yajñavalkya:** cards

SCENE 3

On stage: River bank

SCENE 4

On stage: Dining-table. *On it:* four place settings, glasses etc., candelabra with candles
4, chairs

Off stage: Wine, various dishes etc. **(ffines and Nit)**

Personal: **ffines:** cloth
Mrs Thoroughfare: lorgnon, card

SCENE 5

On stage: Chairs (in the Nook)

Off stage: Pink kite **(Niri-Esther)**

SCENE 6

On Stage: Settee
Small table
Chairs

Valmouth

65

Off stage: Relic, books **(Fowler)**
Tea-tray containing cups, saucers, teapot, sugar, milk etc. **(ffines)**
Pink kite **(Stage Management)**
Kite string **(Niri-Esther)**

Personal: **Mrs Thoroughfare:** book
Mrs Hurstpierpoint: rosary beads

SCENE 7

On stage: Nil

Personal: **Mrs Yajñavalkya:** doctor's bag

SCENE 8

On stage: Daleman statue

Off stage: Basket **(Thetis)**

SCENE 9

On stage: Ornamental shrubs
Flowerbeds
Trees. *Hanging from one:* swing twined with flowers
Trays of drinks etc. **(Nit and ffines)**

Personal: **Mrs Hurstpierpoint:** leaflets

ACT II

SCENE 1

On stage: Ornamental shrubbery
Garden seats
Nude statues
Chair, easel, painting, paints, brushes, etc. (for **Sir Victor**)

Off stage: Perambulator **(Mrs Yajñavalkya)**
Baby wrapped in lace shawl **(Mrs Yajñavalkya)**
Dead, unplucked chickens **(David)**

Personal: **Jack:** book, lighted cigarette, comb
Niri-Esther: flowers
Lady Parvula: chicken feathers

SCENE 2

On stage: River bank

Off stage: Bunch of flowers **(Carry)**

SCENE 3

On stage: Ornamental shrubbery
Garden seats
Nude statues
Canopy over chapel entrance

Off stage: Flowers, prayer-books, plates of sandwiches etc. (**Nit** and **Fowler**)
Baby in long christening robe (**Mrs Hurstpierpoint**)
Religious banner (**Sister Ecclesia**)
Incense-burner (**Nit**)
Parchment with seal (**Father Colley-Mahoney**)

Personal: **Grannie Tooke:** walking stick
Mrs Hurstpierpoint: black mask

SCENE 4

On stage: Nil

SCENE 5

On stage: Perambulator
Baby

Personal: **Mrs Yajñavalkya:** doctor's bag

LIGHTING PLOT

Practical fittings required: fairy lights in trees for Act I, Scene 4

Various interior and exterior fittings

ACT I, SCENE 1. Afternoon

To open: Bright summer sunshine

Cue 1   **Mrs Thoroughfare:** (*ecstatically*) "Oh, but the air, the air!"   (Page 2)
         Fade to Black-out

ACT I, SCENE 2. Early evening

To open: Summer sunshine

Cue 2   **David** exits and **Granny Tooke** goes back into the farmhouse   (Page 12)
         Fade to Black-out

ACT I, SCENE 3. Early evening

To open: Sunshine effect

Cue 3   As **Thetis** finishes Song 5   (Page 14)
         Fade to Black-out

ACT I, SCENE 4. Evening

To open: General interior lighting

Cue 4   **Mrs Thoroughfare:** ". . . is more than grubby . . .!"   (Page 20)
         Fade to Black-out

ACT I, SCENE 5. Afternoon

To open: Full general lighting

Cue 5   As **Niri-Esther** sings Song 12   (Page 24)
         Concentrate lighting on **Niri-Esther** *downstage*

ACT I, SCENE 6. Afternoon

To open: General interior lighting with flashes of lightning

Cue 6   **Mrs Thoroughfare** leaves in a huff   (Page 25)
         Lightning

Cue 7   **Fowler** goes   (Page 26)
         Lightning

Cue 8   **Mrs Hurstpierpoint:** "Thou hast sent me an infidel!"   (Page 28)
            Fade to Black-out

ACT I, Scene 7.   Afternoon

To open: Full general lighting

Cue 9   As the end of Song 14   (Page 29)
            Fade to Black-out

Act I, Scene 8.   Day

To open: Full sunshine effect

Cue 10   **Mrs Yajñavalkya** and **Grannie Tooke** exit   (Page 32)
            Fade to Black-out

ACT I, Scene 9.   Evening

To open: Evening effect, practicals on

No cues

ACT II, Scene 1.   Autumn afternoon

To open: General sunshine effect

Cue 11   **Mrs Thoroughfare** faints again   (Page 50)
            Quick fade to Black-out

ACT II, Scene 2.   Afternoon

To open: General sunshine effect

Cue 12   As **Sister Ecclesia** finishes Song 27A   (Page 54)
            Fade to Black-out

ACT II, Scene 3.   Day

To open: Heavy, overcast effect

Cue 13   **Nit:** "The river is rising!"   (Page 60)
            Fade to Black-out

Act II, Scene 4.   Day

To open: Heavy storm effect

Cue 14   **Lady Parvula:** ". . . caught up with us at last."   (Page 61)
            Flash of lightning

Cue 15   **Mrs Thoroughfare:** "My dear friend!"   (Page 62)
            Fade to Black-out

ACT II, Scene 5.   Day

To open: Brilliant sunshine

EFFECTS PLOT

ACT I

Cue 1	**David:** (*off, shouting*) "To heel! Bad dog!" *Dog barks*	(Page 2)
Cue 2	**Mrs Thoroughfare:** "... extraordinarily extraordinary girl." *Dog barks*	(Page 2)
Cue 3	**Nit:** "How he do press!" *Sound of wheels and horses' hooves*	(Page 14)
Cue 4	To open SCENE 6 *Thunder*	(Page 25)
Cue 5	**Mrs Thoroughfare** leaves in a huff *Thunderclap*	(Page 25)
Cue 6	**Mrs Hurstpierpoint:** "... must be postponed!" *Thunderclap*	(Page 26)
Cue 7	To open SCENE 9 *Sound of conversation etc., continue throughout scene*	(Page 32)
Cue 8	**Niri-Esther:** "Stop!" *Peacock cry*	(Page 36)
Cue 9	**Grannie Tooke:** "... when I was a girl." *Peacock cry*	(Page 37)

ACT II

Cue 10	**David** turns away from **Lady Parvula** in confusion *Peacock cry*	(Page 59)
Cue 11	**Mrs Hurstpierpoint:** "... a feeling of foreboding." *Organ music*	(Page 59)
Cue 12	**Thetis:** "Now you can come back to me!" *Violent thunder*	(Page 60)
Cue 13	**Lady Parvula:** "Heavens, what a débâcle!" *Crash of thunder, torrential rain effect, continue until Lights come up for SCENE 4*	(Page 61)
Cue 14	**Lady Parvula:** "Eulalia is all alone." *Loud thunderclap*	(Page 61)
Cue 15	**Lady Parvula:** "... caught up with us at last." *Crash*	(Page 62)
Cue 16	**Mrs Thoroughfare:** "My dear friend!" *Increase thunder*	(Page 62)

MADE AND PRINTED IN GREAT BRITAIN BY
LATIMER TREND & COMPANY LTD, PLYMOUTH
MADE IN ENGLAND

www.ingramcontent.com/pod-product-compliance
Lightning Source LLC
LaVergne TN
LVHW051800080426
835511LV00018B/3366